Michael Newman speaks the truth in love with empathy and acknowledgment of what happens to a person during grief and loss—emotionally, physically, chemically, spiritually, and relationally. He writes about the reality of life and brings our focus back to our Lord God through Scripture in a nonthreatening way. When one is weakened by grief, he or she can't concentrate on a whole book or a long reading, but these short chapters get right to the point. I recommend this book as a resource for parish nurses, lay ministers, Stephen Ministers, pastors, and others who walk alongside someone experiencing heartbreak.

KAREN HARDECOPF, RN, CERTIFIED LAY MINISTER– PARISH NURSE, STEPHEN MINISTER LEADER

Grief hits us all at various times throughout our lives. This book gives encouragement by taking us on a journey through the lives of people in the Scriptures who grieve, yes, but with the hope that comes from trusting in the God of heaven and earth, the one who rules over life and death, who conquers grief with eternal joy. It is a book to share, but even more importantly, it is a book to read.

REV. DR. GREGORY P. SELTZ, SPEAKER OF THE LUTHERAN HOUR

Michael Newman provides the reader with insight, sensitivity, and encouragement. He consistently shares the love of God and assures us that Jesus understands and cares. His personal style suggests that the author also understands and cares. As a parish nurse, I will use this book with individuals and groups experiencing grief and loss. I also recommend that parish nurses and others involved in congregational health ministry read and discuss in small groups to enhance their compassionate care to the person who is grieving.

MARCIA SCHNORR, EDD, RN-BC, CERTIFIED LAY MINISTER– PARISH NURSE

When looking through a prism, light is refracted into a full spectrum of colors. Michael W. Newman accomplishes the same thing here, treating grief as a prism through which we see the full spectrum of emotions and experiences that loss brings to life. The conversational tone of his writing makes the reader feel as if he has crawled into his or her mind, truly grasping the nuances of grief as one struggles to move from brokenness to healing. Best of all, each and every chapter clearly articulates that we cannot accomplish this on our own, pointing to Jesus Christ as the true source of hope and strength. A must-have for all of us, at any stage of life.
JANE P. WILKE, EDUCATOR, AUTHOR, SPEAKER, ENCOURAGER

WHAT PEOPLE ARE SAYING ABOUT HOPE WHEN YOUR HEART BREAKS

Written from a grace-filled pastor's heart, Michael Newman has penned an essential resource for embracing hope amidst grief. Hope dims when life's storms hit, but Michael skillfully uses Scripture to ignite the torch of healing. His beautiful insights into grief tell us he's been there. He wraps God's words of hope around the grieving like a toasty blanket on a frosty night. Compassionate, crucial, Christ-centered—and critically needed. I will absorb and share this brilliant resource for years to come.
DONNA PYLE, ARTESiAN MINISTRIES, AUTHOR, SPEAKER

Grief is messy. Life after loss doesn't follow an ordered and predictable path, but looks more like a tangled plate of spaghetti. Navigating confusing emotions and thoughts requires a reliable guide, and you've got a friend in Michael W. Newman. Grief is messy, and Michael Newman understands messy. These short chapters explore the untidy realities of what happens after loss. *Hope When Your Heart Breaks* validates the pain of loss, offers helpful insight, and gently points to a Savior who redeems your suffering with purpose and hope. Read and gift this book. You will be comforted and the Holy Spirit will grow your faith.
RUTH N. KOCH, MA, NCC, MENTAL HEALTH EDUCATOR

This is a refreshing book! The Bible is absolutely unique among the sacred writings of all religions. It is the historical description of God's love influencing the lives of real people facing real situations. Michael Newman has taken this unique reality and put it to use in the daily struggles of the Christian. He offers a clear connection between biblical life situations and the reader's daily life. Through it all, he shows the intricate way that God's love is at work in the lives of His people, giving direction and hope to those struggling with difficult emotions and tough situations.
REV. DR. DAVID J. LUDWIG, PASTOR, PROFESSOR, AUTHOR

Michael Newman's book . . . demonstrates a personal and pastoral acquaintance with the gut-wrenching realities of the grief process from a variety of losses—death of a loved one, loss of a job, family crisis, and dramatic changes in the aging process. The issues and questions raised by each chapter strike raw emotions, thoughts, and faith struggles at various stages in the grief process. Each chapter also connects the struggle with biblical narratives and comforting Christ-centered passages, which bring hope to the situation while encouraging the ongoing work of grief. I strongly recommend this book for personal use and for giving to family and friends in need.
REV. DR. STEPHEN J. CARTER, PASTOR, PROFESSOR, AND AUTHOR

There is a reason they call it grief work. This resource honors the process of grief, as well as the value of the loss experience, the tears, the struggle, and the sadness even. It also recognizes the breadth of diversity in the grief experience for each individual. The text is artfully organized so that the readers can pick it up and look through a section that speaks to them, or read through the book as a whole. The insight into the humanity of those who have walked through loss in Scripture is unique and deeply comforting. If you are grieving, if you are walking alongside someone who is grieving, if you are in clinical practice or offer spiritual care, this book is a welcome resource for your shelf!
HEIDI GOEHMANN, DEACONESS, WRITER, BLOGGER, AND SPEAKER AT I LOVE MY SHEPHERD MINISTRIES

Grief is involved in every change in life. Michael Newman understands this and seeks to find the threads of grief that are in life experiences such as fear, anger, depression, guilt, and purposelessness. Each of the fifty-two devotional chapters is independent of the others. The meditation itself will connect with you; devotional guides follow every chapter for further spiritual work; prayer encouragement and direction end each chapter.
BRUCE M. HARTUNG, PHD, PROFESSOR EMERITUS, PRACTICAL THEOLOGY

NAVIGATING GRIEF AND LOSS
MICHAEL W. NEWMAN

Hope

When Your

Heart

Breaks

CONCORDIA PUBLISHING HOUSE · SAINT LOUIS

TO CINDY:
Through blessing
And challenge
With tears
And with joy
We've seen the faithfulness of Jesus
Together

Published 2017 Concordia Publishing House

3558 S. Jefferson Avenue, St. Louis, MO 63118-3968

1-800-325-3040 · www.cph.org

Cover art: Shutterstock

Manufactured in the United States of America

LIBRARY OF CONGRESS CATALOGING-IN-PUBLICATION DATA

Names: Newman, Michael W., 1961- author.

Title: Hope when your heart breaks : navigating grief and loss / Michael W. Newman.

Description: Saint Louis : Concordia Publishing House, [2017] | Includes bibliographical references and index.

Identifiers: LCCN 2017025031 (print) | LCCN 2017032369 (ebook) | ISBN 9780758658609 | ISBN 9780758658562 (alk. paper)

Subjects: LCSH: Consolation. | Grief--Religious aspects--Christianity. | Loss (Psychology)--Religious aspects--Christianity.

Classification: LCC BV4905.3 (ebook) | LCC BV4905.3 .N49 2017 (print) | DDC 248.8/6--dc23

LC record available at https://lccn.loc.gov/2017025031

5   6   7   8   9   10   11   12   28   27   26   25   24   23   22

CONTENTS

How to Use This Book

My prayer for you is that this book can be a place of refuge and a point of reference. You're reading this because you've experienced heartbreak. Grief has entered your life. You've suffered a broken relationship, the loss of a job, a dashed hope and dream, the death of a loved one, or a unique personal experience that has crushed your spirit and caused you pain.

The design of this book lets you find what you need so you can be encouraged and embraced during your loss. Scan through the Contents page and find what speaks to you. No chapter is dependent on another. It is not necessary to read the book from cover to cover. Let the right chapter speak to you at the proper time. Let the wisdom and consolation of the God who pursues you and cares about you help you in your time of need.

Each chapter closes with a reading and some questions for personal reflection and journaling. If you choose to journey through this book with a friend or a group, you can discuss the questions together as you bear one another's burdens and offer one another insight and consolation.

May your reading be blessed. May your walk through grief be filled with welcome surprises of replenishment and restoration. As you navigate your heartbreak, may you discover what you need the most in the midst of grief: **the gift of hope**.

Michael W. Newman

The Beginning
WHEN GRIEF SHOWS UP

And Joseph's master took him and put him into the
prison, the place where the king's prisoners were
confined, and he was there in prison. (Genesis 39:20)

INVADED

It's happened to you, hasn't it? Grief has shown up on your door-
step. This unwelcome visitor has gained access to your life. That's
usually how grief appears on the scene. When you least expect it, an
interloper hacks into your system, breaks into your home, and invades your life. Now you're stuck with an unwanted guest who casts
a dark shadow over your heart, mind, and soul. Grief has settled in.
You feel its oppressive presence, and you don't like it.

It wasn't supposed to be this way, but something broke your
heart. Someone left you feeling empty and numb. A circumstance
became an unpleasant and course–altering surprise. Somehow, in
some way, you have experienced loss—serious and gut–wrenching
loss. With the wind knocked out of you, you wonder if you can keep
going. You wish it wasn't true. You hope it will go away and life will
be like it once was.

IN PRISON

Allow me to introduce you to a person named Joseph. Joseph's
story unfolds in Genesis, the first book of the Bible. Loss was forced
upon Joseph when he was just a kid. Grief shadowed him for decades.
If you're experiencing grief, Joseph—a grief expert—may be someone you need with you on your journey. His story is one of repeated
and heartbreaking loss—but also one of unquenchable hope.

When Joseph was just seventeen years old, he was threatened
with death by ten of his brothers. After his oldest brother, Reuben,
persuaded their angry siblings to spare his life, Joseph was sold as a
slave to a passing group of traders. He was taken far away from his

home to the strange and frightening land of Egypt, where he was purchased as a house servant. Once his father's favorite son who wore a coat of many colors with boastful pride, now Joseph was lost, hurt, and alone. He was forced into a land he did not know, hearing a language he did not understand, and slaving at work he never wanted. Loss was piled upon loss.

Joseph's master was Potiphar, the captain of Pharaoh's guard. Potiphar's wife took a liking to young and handsome Joseph and persisted in trying to persuade him to sleep with her. When Joseph did the right thing and resisted the seductive invitations of his master's wife, he wasn't rewarded for his faithfulness. Instead, Potiphar's wife accused Joseph of making romantic advances. Unjustly accused and with reputation smeared, Joseph was thrown into prison.

There he sat. From the time he was cast into the pit by his brothers to the end of his imprisonment and shame, Joseph languished in loss for thirteen years. That's a long time to feel like you're living in a bad dream, to mourn dashed hopes, to miss what your life once was, and to have a cloud of sadness envelop you every day.

GOD'S PURSUIT

You may feel like you're in a prison as you grieve. You've been unwillingly confined and unjustly held captive. You're in a dark cell with walls pressing in on you. You didn't ask for this claustrophobic darkness. You never wanted this pain. And you'd prefer not to have to endure the journey. But here you are.

Grieving is not easy. It may be the most difficult thing you'll ever do. The emotions, thoughts and feelings saturate your being. They slip out when you least expect them. They overcome you when you thought you were in the clear. As Joseph walked through his grief, there were times when he had to run out of the room to weep uncontrollably. This was a Middle Eastern man—a man who became one of the rulers of Egypt. These men did not break down in tears publicly. They did not show their emotions openly. But such is the pathway of grief.

At each step of the way, however, Joseph was not alone. The prevailing theme of Joseph's story in Genesis 37–50 is not one of crushing loss, but one of God's persistent pursuit of Joseph in his pain. That is the theme of your story too. God pursues you in the prison of your grief. He is tenaciously reaching out to you at this very moment.

At every turn, in darkness and in light, while you're occupied with other things or wrestling with your grief as you lie awake at night, God pursues you with His steadfast love and His strengthening faithfulness. As Psalm 23 articulates beautifully, God is your Good Shepherd who draws you close in order to restore your soul. In this season of loss, you have a Savior who never leaves your side. When you're crumbling in weakness, the One who crumbled in weakness on the cross and rose from the dead—defeating the looming darkness of loss—will carry you. God's promise in Isaiah 46 gets to the heart of the matter: "Even to your old age I am he, and to gray hairs I will carry you. I have made, and I will bear; I will carry and will save" (v. 4). When a season of grief shows up, this is your lifeline. You've already seen how everything else can fail, but God's promise will never fail you. The risen Savior Jesus is proof of an unfailing promise of strength and hope.

SEASONS OF GRIEF

Please be assured, this time in your life is a season. Seasons come and go. Grief doesn't happen as much in orderly stages as it does in the ebb and flow of seasons. You may experience the cold winds of grief for a short time, with a welcome thaw bringing you into a restoring springtime sooner than you ever thought. It may be, however, that the gray skies and bitter chill of grief keep coming around. When you least expect it or when you thought enough time had passed, the clouds roll in, the withered leaves drop to the ground, and a dark coldness grips you once again. Seasons come around more than once.

Grieving is that kind of journey. It can be messy, chaotic, and exhausting. You will walk through dark valleys. You will also see the sun shine its warm and hope-filled rays over the horizon. Sometimes, God will replace your weeping with gladness, and your grief will become a thing of the past. At other times, grief may keep making visits until that day when winter has gone, the leaves never fall, and the tree of life is always in bloom for the complete healing of your soul.

There's one thing you can be sure of here and now: God will pursue you every step of the way. When grief shows up, you do not have to take the journey alone. Jesus walks with you. Because of His love and grace, you can take the journey of grief with certain hope.

WORDS FOR HEALING
Devotion Guide for Chapter One

READ Psalm 30

REFLECT

How do you empathize with the psalmist's words?

How does this psalm teach you to pray as you navigate grief?

What hope do these words give you for your journey of grief?

PRAY verses 9–12 and personalize your need for help and your request for healing.

Feelings

WHEN YOU'RE ANGRY

[The Shunammite said to the prophet Elisha,]
"As the LORD lives and as you yourself live,
I will not leave you." (2 Kings 4:30)

DECEIVED?

Why did I get my hopes up? Why did I get so involved? Why did I let my guard down? Why did I allow myself to become so vulnerable?

Those may be questions you're asking as your heart aches with loss. You feel betrayed. You feel angry with yourself for being taken in. Or you may be angry with the person who got you into this mess. How could someone raise your hopes and then inflict so much pain? How could someone abandon you? Why would someone take advantage of you and leave you empty, hurting, and alone? It's humiliating and unfair. "Never again," you may say. "I won't go there anymore. I won't let anyone—including God—lead me down a path that will only leave me heartbroken, disappointed, and feeling like a fool. Never again."

It's normal to put up walls during heartbreak. A reaction of anger—at yourself, at someone else, or at a situation—is a natural response. Anger lets you feel your wounds, express your grief, and reassess your boundaries. Anger grabs your heart and drags you into facing your loss whether you want to or not. But anger can be hazardous to handle. Give anger too much leeway in your life, and you can end up lashing out carelessly at people you love. Hold on to anger for too long, and you can end up mired in a festering inner toxicity that withers your heart and robs your soul. So, how can you navigate the anger you feel? What do you do when rage and resentment bring you to tears or begin to boil over into bitterness?

HANGING ON

A woman from Shunem may be the helper you need. She understood the despair and anger of wrenching and unfair loss. She and her husband were blessed with wealth. They extended kindness and hospitality to the prophet Elisha whenever he passed through their region—the region of Shunem. After being blessed by this selfless couple for so long, Elisha wondered how he could repay them. Seeing that this dear woman had no son, Elisha said to her one day, "At this season, about this time next year, you shall embrace a son" (2 Kings 4:16).

That may sound like good news, but to this woman, the statement from Elisha struck a sensitive nerve. She replied, "No, my lord, O man of God; do not lie to your servant" (v. 16). She may have been saying, "This is a place you shouldn't go, Elisha. My husband and I have been struggling with this for a long time. This is a sore spot. Don't get my hopes up. I don't think about this anymore."

But by spring of the next year, the woman from Shunem had borne a son. Everything was going fine for years. The boy grew. His parents loved him. The family was close. This was an unexpected dream come true—until one random and crushing day. The beloved son went to visit his father as he worked in the fields around his home. Suddenly, the boy complained of a headache. He was rushed home to his mother, where he sat on her lap until noon. Then the unthinkable and senseless happened: the boy died.

Immediately, the woman went to Elisha. She fell before him and grasped his feet. As his servant tried to push her away, Elisha said, "Leave her alone, for she is in bitter distress" (v. 27). The woman said to Elisha, "Did I ask my lord for a son? Did I not say, 'Do not deceive me?' " (v. 28).

She was wounded and angry. She didn't ask for this roller coaster ride of grief. She didn't want to be set up for loss, but here she was. What did she do? Did she stand up and punch Elisha in the nose? Did she give him a tongue-lashing he would never forget? Did she ban him from Shunem and from her house? No, she kept hanging on to his feet and said, "As the LORD lives and as you yourself live, I will not leave you" (v. 30). She hung on to her only hope.

GOD'S AVAILABILITY

Psalm 4 says, "Be angry, and do not sin; ponder in your own hearts on your beds, and be silent. Offer right sacrifices, and put your trust in the LORD" (vv. 4–5). Anger is an emotion, not a sin. But before anger swallows you up and causes you to hurt yourself or others, God offers you a lifeline. You see it in the woman from Shunem. The way to navigate anger is to hang on to your only hope.

God lets you hang on to Him. The Creator of the universe, the Ruler of all humanity, makes Himself available to you. Just as Elisha didn't shoo away the woman from Shunem, God never closes His door in your face. He never blocks your calls, ignores your pleas, or tells you He's busy. In fact, He draws you close—even when you are in bitter distress. God invites you to "cast your burden" on Him (Psalm 55:22; 1 Peter 5:7). That literally means you can throw everything you've got at Him—your anxiety, your anger, your worries, your burdens, and your bitterness. Your Savior is the best place to go when you feel like you have nowhere to turn. God loves you—even when you're not very lovable. You don't have to lash out at others or yourself; you can hang on to Him for hope. In your anger, you can pray and plead with God. As you fume in wounded distress, you are welcomed by God with open arms to pour out your soul and bring Him your complaints. In your haze of questions and confusion, you are embraced by the One who is your help in times of trouble and pain. Anger is a turbulent and terrible place to reside, but God promises to be your abiding hope in that neighborhood of pain.

Elisha answered the woman's pain by miraculously raising her son from the dead. You may not be able to go back to the way it was, but God will take you forward in His grace. You may not see the restoration of what you've lost, but you will see Him who is the resurrection and the life. After all, as the apostle Paul reassured us in Romans 8, "He who did not spare His own Son but gave Him up for us all, how will He not also with Him graciously give us all things?" (v. 32). When you're angry, you can bring all you've got to your Savior and trust in Him. When you experience a gaping hole in your heart, you can hang on. God's outstretched arm of rescue is reaching out to you right now.

WORDS FOR HEALING

Devotion Guide for Chapter Two

READ Psalm 37:1–9

REFLECT

King David wrote this psalm. What evidence do you see of his struggle with loss that leads to frustration and anger?

What counsel and direction for dealing with anger does David give in almost every verse?

What promises about God's gracious action stand out to you in this section of Scripture?

PRAY about the ways anger may be affecting you. Ask God to keep you from sin and to strengthen you in hanging on to Him.

Feelings

WHEN YOU'RE SAD, VERY SAD

Jesus wept. (John 11:35)

THE IMPORTANCE OF SADNESS

What is bringing you to tears these days? When do you feel like crying? You may not like to let the tears flow. After all, having a runny nose and puffy eyes and choking up while trying to have a normal conversation are not social moments to which you aspire. But there is a reason for your tears. Your tears show your heart. And you shouldn't hold back.

A number of years ago, Captain Richard Phillips was taken captive by pirates when they tried to commandeer his ship during a voyage off the coast of Africa. Phillips suffered fear, physical abuse, and emotional turmoil during his hostage ordeal. He thought he would lose everything and everyone at the hands of the criminals who held him. A daring rescue by U.S. Navy SEALs gave Phillips freedom and a new lease on life, but the trauma remained. The first night after the rescue, Captain Phillips woke up weeping. He said to himself, "What am I? A wimp? I'm lucky to be alive, and here I am crying like a girl." But the next morning, the same thing happened. Out of a deep sleep, he found himself sobbing. Phillips was strongly encouraged to talk to the Navy psychiatrist onboard his rescue ship bound for a safe haven. His first reaction was, "I'm not really into nut doctors." Finally he relented, and the conversation with the doctor was truly enlightening. The doctor told Phillips that when a person experiences a crisis, the body releases chemicals to help it cope. These hormones course through a person's system and need to be released. The doctor asked Captain Phillips if he was experiencing episodes of crying. Phillips was surprised that the doctor knew exactly what he was going through. Then the doctor asked how he was handling it. Phillips replied, "I yell at myself, tell myself to stop being a wimp, splash water on my face, and get over it." The doctor replied, "Next time, don't end it. Just let it run its course."

So Captain Phillips let the tears flow. The next morning, when waves of grief awakened him, he didn't hold back. He leaned into the sadness. He embraced his raw emotion. For thirty minutes straight, he sat on the edge of his bed, put his head in his hands, and cried (adapted from Richard Phillips and Stephan Talty, *A Captain's Duty* [New York: Hyperion, 2011], 273–74).

Captain Phillips's first step in dealing with profound sadness may be the step you need to take. Physically, emotionally, and spiritually, you may need to be sad. As you experience loss, it is extremely important for you to acknowledge the importance of what you're feeling. You are not a random and anonymous collection of cells on a big planet called Earth. You are a person—a unique and precious individual in the eyes of God. You have a heart, and what you experience matters. That's why you need to acknowledge your sadness. That's why you have permission to shed tears. It happens to human beings—even to Jesus, the Son of God.

TEARS

What did Jesus do when He found Himself in your shoes? How did Jesus respond to heartbreak, grief, and loss? Sometimes, Jesus needed to be alone. At other times, He prayed. There were instances when Jesus was moved in His heart to show compassionate action. The Messiah even exhibited flashes of anger. But one consistent response from Jesus in the face of heartbreak is one you may understand very well: Jesus felt sadness; He cried.

We're told it happened more than once: "In the days of His flesh, Jesus offered up prayers and supplications, with loud cries and tears, to Him who was able to save Him from death" (Hebrews 5:7). The tears flowed as Jesus faced a frightening future. They also welled up when His heart broke for the people who rejected the grace, life, and eternal hope He offered. The Gospel writer Luke says, "And when [Jesus] drew near and saw [Jerusalem], He wept over it, saying, 'Would that you, even you, had known on this day the things that make for peace! But now they are hidden from your eyes'" (Luke 19:41–42). Jesus wept. You may recognize that famous biblical phrase from Jesus' reaction of deep sadness when He found Himself at His friend's funeral. Lazarus, the brother of Mary and Martha, had died. The Gospel of John recounts: "Now when Mary came to where Jesus was and saw Him, she fell at His feet, saying to Him, 'Lord, if You had been here, my brother would not have died.' When Jesus saw her weeping, and the Jews who had come with her also weeping, He was deeply moved in His spirit and greatly troubled. And He said, 'Where have you laid him?' They said to Him, 'Lord, come and see.' Jesus wept" (John 11:32–35).

Jesus' tears showed His heart. And He didn't hold back.

THE BEGINNING OF JOY

You are blessed when you have such high hopes and such meaningful love that loss leads to tears. You're not a wimp when you cry. You're not weak when you feel sad. You're not defective when you become despondent. Becoming vulnerable because of tears is not a threat to your pride, it's a window to your heart. You've taken the risk of living, and even though life bruises and injures you, your scars and sorrow bear testimony to the love and passion you invest every day.

But sadness does not mean you're without hope.

King Solomon's wisdom provides encouragement when he comments in Ecclesiastes 7:3, "Sorrow is better than laughter, for by sadness of face the heart is made glad." Your sadness honors your love, your hopes, your dreams, and your relationships. Sadness needs to run its course because, as Solomon knew, tears will not hold you captive in sadness; they will free you for a future of joy and gladness. That is the counterintuitive beauty of God's grace. And that is why Jesus weeps with you. Like you, He cries real tears. He lets you know that your life is of utmost importance to Him. And at the right time, He will show you the joy that awaits you on the other side of sadness.

WORDS FOR HEALING
Devotion Guide for Chapter Three

READ Psalm 77:1–12

REFLECT

How do verses 1–3 help you embrace your own sadness?

How do you relate to the feelings and questions in verses 4–9?

What encouragement, hope, and direction do verses 10–12 provide?

PRAY about your sadness—pour out your feelings to God. Then thank Him for His good and mighty deeds. Let Him know how you've seen Him come through for you. Ask Him to help you trust Him to come through again.

Feelings
WHEN YOU FEEL HELPLESS

The angel of the LORD came again a second time
and touched [Elijah] and said, "Arise and eat, for
the journey is too great for you." (1 Kings 19:7)

HITTING THE WALL

It is not easy to come to the searing realization that there is absolutely nothing you can do. Staying awake all night doesn't help. Turning over the "what-ifs" in your mind doesn't make a difference. No matter how much you wish or how hard you try, you can't rewind your life. You're not able to go back and make adjustments. What happened is done. And when what happened breaks your heart, you feel dejected and stuck. You're helpless.

Grief and loss are persistently and surprisingly shocking because no matter how much experience you gain in suffering, new heartbreak keeps breaking your heart. It lays you low. It makes you weak. Very quickly, you realize that you can't think yourself out of your grief. Denial won't keep it at bay. Anger doesn't overpower it. Talent and creativity won't make it disappear.

At some point on your journey of grief, you may resemble a person named Elijah. After running away, concocting a plan, expending personal energy, and experiencing an emotional crash of despair, Elijah collapsed in exhaustion and asked God to take his life. He said, "I've had enough, Lord." The mighty and bold prophet of God finally hit the wall of his own strength and ability. He couldn't do this on his own.

GOD'S WHISPERER

That is not an easy fact to admit. Not stopping to ask for directions is legendary fodder for arguments between husbands and wives. Men don't like to ask for help. Young children are renowned for pushing parental assistance away as they declare, "I want to do it myself!" Women have been known to collapse in tears and exhaustion before inviting someone to help with an important project or with everything necessary to prepare for guests. We can be as stubborn as mules as we march forward to our own destruction.

That is why God, in His understanding and grace, sent His angel to whisper into Elijah's ear, "The journey is too great for you" (1 Kings 19:7). In addition to His whisper, God sent provisions. He prepared food for Elijah. Twice, as Elijah lay exhausted and depressed under a broom tree, God prepared fresh baked bread and thirst-quenching water for the exhausted and beleaguered prophet. The bushy wilderness tree brought shade. The fresh food and water brought strength. The gentle touch and whisper brought the truth: the journey *was* too much for Elijah. He couldn't tackle the rigors of life on his own.

It's no different for you and me. Elijah was being threatened by a seething Queen Jezebel. He may have been regretting the way he commandeered control over hundreds of the queen's pagan prophets. You may be regretting something you did before your heartbreak hit. You may be afraid that your future or the future of someone you love is ruined. You may feel that you have nowhere to turn and there is nothing you can do. If you're in that fragile place, I have news for you: God has you exactly where He wants you. In that place, you'll hear Him whisper: "The journey is too great for you." At this moment, you will come to one of the most important realizations of your life: you desperately need God's help. You can't tackle the harsh reality or the rigors of life on your own.

HELP WHEN YOU NEED IT MOST

Please know that as you lie in the wilderness of your own helplessness, God whispers to your heart through His powerful Word. He sets a table and prepares a banquet. He serves up the bread of life. He pours out His living water. He shelters you in the shadow of the cross. Jesus, the Helper of the helpless, does what you cannot do. Jesus, the Finder of the lost, meets you when you have nowhere to turn. Jesus, the Forgiver of the fallen, redeems your past and sets you on a new path in life. The old is gone; the new has come.

Look what happened to poor Elijah. Two helpings of God's nourishment gave him strength to travel forty days and forty nights to the mountain of God. God's gracious help in the midst of helplessness brought a disheartened prophet into the presence of divine compassion and counsel. Elijah cried out, "I have been very jealous for the LORD, the God of hosts. For the people of Israel have forsaken Your covenant, thrown down Your altars, and killed Your prophets with the sword, and I, even I only, am left, and they seek my life, to take it away" (1 Kings 19:10). God listened patiently to Elijah's persistent complaint. Then, He lifted Elijah up, dusted him off, and gave him a glimpse of a much bigger picture of very present grace. Two kings would be appointed to accomplish God's mission. A prophet would be raised up to take the burden of leadership from Elijah. And even though he felt alone, Elijah was not on his own. God revealed a crowd of seven thousand fellow followers of the true God who remained strong in faith.

You will face moments when you are absolutely helpless. Contrary to the motivational rally cry that you can do anything you put your mind to, there will be frightening instances when you realize your complete powerlessness. During those times, when the journey is too great for you, the life-restoring whisper of God can reverberate in your soul: "God is our refuge and strength, a very present help in trouble" (Psalm 46:1). Fed by the nourishment of God's Word, you will go far. Refreshed by the water of Baptism, you will never have to rely on your stamina alone. Accompanied by your Refuge and Strength, your helplessness will become a vantage point for God's grace. He will show you the bigger picture of His caring, comforting, renewing, reassuring, strengthening, and steadfast love.

WORDS FOR HEALING
Devotion Guide for Chapter Four

READ Psalm 46

REFLECT

How are mountains trembling and waters roaring as you face instability and helplessness in your life these days?

What comfort and encouragement do you find in verses 4–9?

Verse 10 begins, "Be still, and know that I am God." How is God calming you and strengthening you lately?

PRAY about how God might be exalted even through your struggle. Let God know why you're thankful that He is with you and is your fortress.

Feelings
WHEN YOU FEEL DISPLACED

I, Daniel, perceived in the books the number of years
that, according to the word of the LORD to Jeremiah the
prophet, must pass before the end of the desolations of
Jerusalem, namely, seventy years. Then I turned my face to
the Lord God, seeking Him by prayer and pleas for mercy
with fasting and sackcloth and ashes. (Daniel 9:2–3)

UPROOTED

You may not like where you are right now. The heartbreak you've
experienced may have put you in a place you would rather not be.
You never thought you would find yourself in this situation. You
never imagined you would be forced to bear this new identity. You
never wanted this unpleasant struggle. But here you are, displaced
and uprooted.

It's not a good feeling. It is very difficult to come to grips with life
in a foreign land. Suddenly, you have a new set of unwelcome worries
and fears. You have to explain your circumstances. You are in the
uncomfortable position of helping people see through the extra layer
of haze that obscures your real identity. Or you may just clam up and
say nothing—let them figure it out on their own. Life has become
very complicated, but you don't want the complication. Your reality
is different now, different in a wrong and disheartening way. If only
you could go home—back to the way it once was, or immediately out
of this "vale of tears" to be with God. Either way, you want out of
your "Babylon."

Babylon is a place of captivity. A boy named Daniel was taken
from his home to that place of unwanted confinement. Daniel was
just a teen when his life was interrupted and he was carted off to
a foreign land. Before his existence was forcefully changed, Daniel
probably looked forward to an exciting future. He was the son of no-
bility and had the world at his fingertips. No doubt, this handsome

and strong boy would marry a lovely girl and have a fulfilling life as one of Israel's leaders. But that was not to be. In a violent and shocking turn, Daniel was torn from all familiarity and cut off from the future he imagined and hoped for. With his homeland overrun by Babylonian warriors, Daniel was kidnapped, brought to Babylon, and forced to serve the whims of cruel King Nebuchadnezzar.

Daniel was displaced. He never asked for the life he now had. He didn't want to be in this situation. He had no desire or motivation to function in his new identity or role. Daniel wanted to be home. He wanted his life back. The Bible recounts that, after languishing in a foreign land for nearly seventy years, Daniel showed how uncomfortable and uprooted he felt. He fell on his face in prayer and pleaded with God to restore Jerusalem and to let him and his people go home. He said, "O Lord, hear; O Lord, forgive. O Lord, pay attention and act. Delay not, for Your own sake, O my God, because Your city and Your people are called by Your name" (Daniel 9:19).

YOUR BABYLON

You may feel like Daniel. You want your life back. You want to feel at home. Instead of discomfort and awkwardness and pain, you want your heartbreak to disappear so you can be at peace and live normally once again. But loss doesn't always work that way.

Daniel never got to go home. He endured at least seven decades of unwanted displacement. How did Daniel make it through the ups and downs of life in Babylon—and how can you? First, with the gift of prayer. When corrupt leaders coerced the king into signing a law that punished anyone who offered a prayer to someone other than the king himself, what did Daniel do? "When Daniel knew that the document had been signed, he went to his house where he had windows in his upper chamber open toward Jerusalem. He got down on his knees three times a day and prayed and gave thanks before his God, as he had done previously" (Daniel 6:10). It got him thrown into a den of lions, but Daniel prayed. He kept going back to a relationship of trust and dependence on God. And throughout every step of Daniel's perilous journey, God responded by showing His faithful care and rescue.

Second, Daniel made it through his displacement by standing on a foundation of God's promises. Daniel grew in his faith by reading the Scriptures. He searched God's Word as a lifeline of certainty in an uncertain place. Ultimately, he had faith in the words God spoke, that those who trust in God's wisdom "shall shine like the brightness of the sky above; and those who turn many to righteousness, like the stars forever and ever" (Daniel 12:3).

You may not have the future you once thought about and longed for. You may now be experiencing an unpleasant new reality. But God gives you the lifeline of prayer and the foundation of His promises. As you live in your Babylon, you have not lost your freedom to call upon the One who never leaves you nor forsakes you. The opportunity to pour out your soul to your Savior in prayer and to wait for His wisdom and response is more important now than ever. Prayer is your lifeline, and God's Word is your solid foundation. More than ever, the restoring reassurance of God's promises forms the bedrock you need for a shaken life. Read, listen, and be renewed.

Sometimes, captivity can bring great clarity. Instead of idolizing your life, you begin to understand your purpose. Instead of relying on your fragile strength, you are led to seek refuge in God's faithful solutions. Daniel's displaced presence in Babylon brought God's light and truth to a dark and deceived world. Your Babylon may need what you have to offer. God may have you exactly where He needs you—even if it means sharing in His suffering.

You see, that is the pathway of your Savior Jesus. He was displaced. The Son of God became a servant, humbling Himself even to the point of death on a cross. He entered the foreign territory of this broken world to save you. Because of Jesus, no matter how uprooted you feel, your identity is never lost and you are never alone. You always have someone who understands you; you are never without hope; and you always have a treasure to share.

WORDS FOR HEALING
Devotion Guide for Chapter Five

READ Psalm 102:1–13

REFLECT

This psalm is "A Prayer of one afflicted." What feelings and thoughts do you relate to most in these verses?

Verse 10 expresses the imagery of being cast aside by God. How does your displacement make you feel forgotten by God?

What hope do verses 12–13 provide?

PRAY for God's help and peace as you face your "Babylon." Ask Jesus to show you compassion, to give you strength, and to use you for His saving purpose as you journey through a new reality.

Feelings
WHEN YOU FEEL LIKE IT'S ALL YOUR FAULT

Jacob said, "I will not let You go unless
You bless me." (Genesis 32:26)

REGRET

"If only . . ." Those two small words can bring gigantic waves of
guilt into your life. If only you had controlled your temper. If only
you had seen the warning signs. If only you had not taken so much
for granted. If only you had listened to the counsel of friends. If only
you had acted earlier. If only you had treasured the time you had. If
only you had been more responsible. If only.

As each "if only" piles up, your burden grows and a sense of shame
can begin to develop. You may be tempted to become self-critical, believing you're irretrievably flawed and becoming convinced that your
guilt has no remedy.

Heartbreak can do that to you. Not only does it wound you to
the core, it can expose every weakness and failure. It breaks you wide
open and puts you at risk. It takes a heaping helping of blame and
dishes it up into your psyche and soul.

WRESTLING

That's why you need to meet Jacob, the son of Isaac and grand-
son of Abraham. Jacob's exploits fill the pages of the first book of
the Bible, Genesis. From the beginning, Jacob was stirring up trouble. He wrestled with his twin brother, Esau, in their mother's womb.
He was born in a competitive posture, grasping at Esau's heel. That's
how he got his name. *Jacob* means "he grasps the heel," an expression
of his slick, aggressive, and deceptive style. After he grew up, Jacob
kept scheming for the advantage. He stole Esau's birthright when his
brother was hungry and vulnerable. He fooled his father into giving
him Esau's blessing—the rights and privileges of the firstborn son
in the family. Of course, Esau was furious. Genesis 27:41 gives us

the gory details: "Now Esau hated Jacob because of the blessing with which his father had blessed him, and Esau said to himself, 'The days of mourning for my father are approaching; then I will kill my brother Jacob.' "

Why all the talk about Jacob? Because the point came in his life when he became plagued by "if onlys." After twenty years of life on the lam from angry and vengeful Esau, God told Jacob to return home. Starting to feel the heavy weight of guilt for all his misdeeds, Jacob sent word to Esau that he was coming back. Esau responded by gathering four hundred men and marching toward his deceptive and conniving twin. The Bible says, "Jacob was greatly afraid and distressed" (Genesis 32:7). Immediately, Jacob began to pray. That night, alone in the wilderness, we're told that Jacob wrestled with God. And it is this wrestling match that reveals the reason for your hope when you feel like it's all your fault.

Jacob wrestled with every regret. He turned over in his mind every reason for guilt. He agonized about his faults and beat himself up for the harm he caused. But as he encountered God that awful and frightening day, Jacob wouldn't give up. He didn't let go. Even though he knew he wasn't deserving of any of God's favor or help, he refused to believe anything but God's promise of love and faithfulness. As dawn broke, Jacob said to God, "I will not let You go unless You bless me." So God blessed him. He gave Jacob a new name. He called him "Israel," which means "you have [contended] with God and with men, and have prevailed" (Genesis 32:28).

That is your answer when you are haunted by guilt and regret. Your failures may have been significant. Your faults may be real and wreckage causing. The guilt you feel in the midst of grief and loss may be something you're afraid to discuss, but it stays close and haunts your soul. That's why God stays with you in your wrestling match. Being sinful, flawed, and wrong doesn't mean you have to abandon hope in God's desire to stick with you. In fact, you can hang on to Him and insist on His blessing. You can be assured that because of His great mercy and grace, your Savior will give you a new name, a new beginning. He will forgive you and release you into a new season of life.

RENEWAL

You see, God's grace isn't hindered by your failures. It's actually present because of them. That's the promise Jacob clung to. It's the promise that can serve as an anchor for your soul as well. The unique and life-restoring work of Jesus is revealed in Isaiah 53, "Surely He has borne our griefs and carried our sorrows; yet we esteemed Him stricken, smitten by God, and afflicted. But He was pierced for our transgressions; He was crushed for our iniquities; upon Him was the chastisement that brought us peace, and with His wounds we are healed" (Isaiah 53:4–5). Jesus shouldered all your faults and put them to death on the cross. When He rose to life, your wounds were healed and your life was renewed. Now, like Jacob, you can walk toward home in the grace of God.

Be aware, however, that your walk may be a little different. After his wrestling match with God, Jacob limped. It showed everybody that he was a changed person. It will happen to you too. God's goodness will give you a different gait. It's called walking in repentance. Esau noticed Jacob's new sense of humility and compassion. When he and his brother finally met, Esau ran and embraced Jacob. Your renewed life will be noticeable too. Heartbreak will humble you, but God's grace will strengthen you. Your Savior is with you every step of the way. Today you can take heart; grief will never break you. It can never extinguish your hope.

WORDS FOR HEALING
Devotion Guide for Chapter Six

READ Psalm 51:1–13

REFLECT

How do these verses get to the heart of the guilt you feel?

What message of hope and renewal do verses 7–12 give?

How does verse 13 fit into the new life given to you by faith in Jesus?

PRAY verses 10–12, bringing the guilt that plagues you to God, refusing to let go of His promise of mercy, and asking Him to bless you in the ways you need it most.

Feelings

WHEN YOU FEEL LIKE YOU WANT TO DISAPPEAR

[Jesus said,] "Martha, Martha, you are anxious and
troubled about many things." (Luke 10:41)

AWKWARD

Heartbreak can be humiliating. When hurt hits you, it often
takes place in a public way. People knew your situation before life
came crashing down; now they know your new reality. They may not
be aware of all the details, but they see without a doubt that something has changed. So the questions start to come. What happened?
Why? Some people offer input. Some try to help but say the wrong
thing. Others back off as if you're to blame. Some try to get you to
brush it off.

Loss can put you into the awkward and uncomfortable position
of dreading conversations, questions, and encounters with people
you know. It can make you feel like you want to disappear. When
you're barely able to process the rejection you've experienced, you
are put in the embarrassing position of reviewing the events publicly.
What do you say? What do you do?

You don't feel like showing your face in public. You don't want
to go anywhere. You definitely don't want to look at social media.
How can you respond? Will you be able to maintain your composure?
Should you defend yourself? Do you need to explain what happened?

PUBLIC HUMILIATION

Those were questions Mary may have been harboring in her
wounded heart in Luke 10. As Jesus journeyed with His disciples, He
was invited into Mary's home. She lived with her sister, Martha, and
her brother, Lazarus. We're told that, after Jesus was welcomed into
their home, Mary sat at Jesus' feet and listened to His teaching. Who
wouldn't? Who could resist soaking in the pearls of wisdom spoken
by the Son of God? Who could put time listening to Jesus at the
bottom of a priority list? The One who fed the five thousand, calmed

the storm, healed the sick, and raised the dead probably had some compelling things to share. So Mary gave her rapt attention to Him who spoke with both authority and compassion.

But Martha begged to differ. We are told that "Martha was distracted with much serving. . . . She went up to [Jesus] and said, 'Lord, do You not care that my sister has left me to serve alone? Tell her to help me' " (Luke 10:40). Martha threw her sister under the bus! She called her out in front of the Holy Son of God. She embarrassed her in front of the Messiah. She politely implied that Mary was lazy and irresponsible. She gave the strong public impression that Mary was incorrigible and could only be straightened out if Jesus lent a rebuking hand.

That's when you want to disappear. Life gets all too public. You can't grieve your loss privately. It has to be in front of the whole world. You can't navigate your heartbreak quietly. People keep bringing it up. You can't work through your rejection personally. Somebody is always curiously awaiting the latest update. And when all eyes are turned upon you, dread and shame well up inside.

So there Mary sat, looking back and forth between her loudmouthed sister and Jesus. The moment may have seemed like an eternity of embarrassment. But then something amazing happened. Jesus spoke up.

OUR ADVOCATE

Martha told Jesus the next step He should take, but Jesus wasn't taken in by Martha's worries and control. Jesus sees a bigger picture and seeks a greater purpose. Martha may have been preparing lunch, but Jesus was preparing an eternal banquet. Martha railed at Mary's fault, but Jesus rejoiced in Mary's faith. So, He answered Martha.

To Mary, it may not have even mattered what Jesus said. In her split second of utter humiliation, Jesus didn't let the feeling linger. He didn't hesitate or allow the awkwardness to prevail. Before Mary's face could become flush with hurt feelings, Jesus filled the gap. He leaped to her defense, stepped in to help, and showed He cared. At what appeared to be the point of her greatest failure, Mary saw the Son of God advocating for her.

He does the same for you. You may feel like you want to disappear, but Jesus insists on being your companion when you are most vulnerable. He calls you a worthy friend. The apostle John knew what it was like to be brushed off and embarrassed. But he also knew Jesus. Later in his life, John reflected honestly about sin and failure. He said, "If anyone does sin, we have an advocate with the Father, Jesus Christ the righteous" (1 John 2:1). We have an advocate. John experienced Jesus' caring defense. Mary did too. When Jesus Christ the Righteous One speaks up for you, there's no one who can speak against you.

THE ELEPHANT IN THE ROOM

Keeping her close, Jesus vindicated vulnerable Mary. He said, "Martha, Martha, you are anxious and troubled about many things, but one thing is necessary. Mary has chosen the good portion, which will not be taken away from her" (Luke 10:41–42).

The elephant in the room disappeared because Jesus said it did not matter. The worries, the judgments, the critical gazes, the fears, and the questions about what people will think don't matter when you sit at your Savior's feet. God's Word says it clearly and emphatically: "There is therefore now no condemnation for those who are in Christ Jesus" (Romans 8:1). Your sin has no consequence because of the cross. Only one thing is necessary: Jesus, the living Word. Do you hear Him? He says, "I am with you always." For your ongoing provision and help, He reassures, "I am the bread of life." To guide you, He directs, "I am the light of the world." To help you, He says, "I am the good shepherd." For your eternal hope, He provides the Good News, "I am the resurrection and the life." For every moment, He says, "I am the way and the truth and the life."

Jesus' voice is the one thing needed amid the confusing voices of your heartbreak. Remaining close to your Savior is the one thing needed when you feel like you want to disappear. Jesus wants to see you next to Him, showing the world what is most important. And with Jesus close, your critics cannot win. With His great and gracious hope, you never have to hide.

WORDS FOR HEALING

Devotion Guide for Chapter Seven

READ Psalm 27:1–5

REFLECT

What does God say in verses 1–3 about the forces that make you want to disappear?

What does it mean for you to have the Lord as your light, as your salvation, and as the stronghold of your life?

Verses 4–5 describe the blessing of being "hidden" by God. How do these verses fill you with hope?

PRAY verses 4–5, asking God to shelter you from harm, to defend you from humiliation, and to allow you to shine His light. Thank Him for the ways He is showing His closeness to you.

Feelings

WHEN YOU FEEL CAST ASIDE

So it went on year by year. (1 Samuel 1:7)

IT'S PERSONAL

"Please don't take this personally." How many times have you heard that phrase in the context of utter rejection? You were hoping for something. You were depending on the answer "yes." You were certain something good would happen. The future looked firm. Your prospects seemed positive. Then the bottom dropped out. Worst of all, as a real and living person, you feel cast aside. You're personally wounded. Maybe you weren't good enough. Maybe you didn't fit in. Maybe there was a better option. Usually you don't receive a satisfactory explanation. Typically, your rejection doesn't make any sense at all. And it feels very personal to lose what you thought was meant to be.

Life is very personal, after all. You can't live as if nothing really matters. You don't invest yourself in hopes and dreams in a cool and detached way. You don't enter relationships holding back your feelings just in case the other person backs out. If you have a heartbeat and are involved in the adventure called "life," there are some areas where you simply have to go all in. It's in those areas where your heart is at high risk. When rejection happens or your hopes don't materialize, it hurts. It's personal.

THE ANGUISH OF REJECTION

The searing pain of rejection comes through clearly in the life of a woman named Hannah. She described herself this way: "I am a woman troubled in spirit. . . . I have been pouring out my soul before the LORD. . . . I have been speaking out of my great anxiety and vexation" (1 Samuel 1:15–16). The words Hannah spoke communicated her heartbreak. "Troubled" is rooted in a Hebrew word that means "hard, difficult, and heavy." "Vexation" points to provocation to the point of anger. Hannah was at her wit's end because of rejection.

What triggered her anguish? Hannah struggled with infertility. Worse than that, she was criticized for not being able to bear a child. In Old Testament days, when men had multiple wives, Hannah found herself pitted against her husband's second wife. We're told, "Her rival used to provoke her grievously to irritate her, because the LORD had closed her womb. So it went on year by year. As often as she went up to the house of the LORD, she used to provoke her. Therefore Hannah wept and would not eat" (1 Samuel 1:6–7). The other wife had children, and she rubbed salt in Hannah's wounded heart for not being able to bear a little one.

Your rejection circumstances may be much different, but being cut off from where you placed your hopes is confusing, agonizing, and annoying. You start to wonder what in the world God is doing. When you feel cast aside, it's usually from something that seems very good and pleasing to God. Why would He say no? The timing seems right. The situation seems appropriate. Why, then, the unexpected and hurtful turn?

THE ANSWER

I don't know. I've been there, and I just don't know why it has to happen the way it does. But I do know one thing: "The LORD is near to the brokenhearted and saves the crushed in spirit" (Psalm 34:18). You may feel cast aside, but God is still very close to you. You may feel alone and ignored, but Jesus is right by your side. You may feel like you have no hope and no future, but "The angel of the LORD encamps around those who fear Him, and delivers them" (Psalm 34:7). God sets up shop where you feel most abandoned. That may be better than what you wanted in the first place.

Hannah discovered that truth. As time went on, God heard Hannah's prayers and gave her a son. She named him Samuel. Before she knew she would have a baby, Hannah vowed to give her child to God's service for life. After Samuel was born and was old enough to begin his service in the temple, she brought him there and presented him to Eli the priest. How could Hannah give away what she hoped for most? She realized that God's closeness is what sustained her, not the attainment of her dream. Your sadness doesn't make you feel abandoned; being sad without a Savior does. Hannah met her Savior in her anguish. His comfort and restoration made her whole.

God never rejects you. Nothing will separate you from His love. The certain words of Romans 8 underscore that God will not cast you aside—even if you feel as though He has: "For I am sure that neither death nor life, nor angels nor rulers, nor things present nor things to come, nor powers, nor height nor depth, nor anything else in all creation, will be able to separate us from the love of God in Christ Jesus our Lord" (Romans 8:38–39). No loss or rejection you suffer indicates abandonment by God. He is committed to you for the long haul. He will never leave you nor forsake you (Deuteronomy 31:6, 8).

HANDLING REJECTION

But how can you keep your confidence and equilibrium in the face of rejection? How can you weather the storm of feeling cast aside? I know the answer to that question: one step at a time. In the context of rejection and the fear of being abandoned, Psalm 37 counsels: "Wait for the LORD and keep His way, and He will exalt you to inherit the land" (v. 34). For each moment, through each thought, as you reflect on what happened and wonder about the future, wait for the Lord and keep His way. Measure each step you take against the goodness and grace of God. Trust Him. He's trustworthy and good as you face rejection, because He has been there. He taught His disciples, "The Son of Man must suffer many things and be rejected by the elders and the chief priests and the scribes and be killed, and after three days rise again" (Mark 8:31). Jesus faced rejection. He acknowledged that rejection would be a hallmark of His life when He applied the words of Psalm 118:22 to Himself, "The stone that the builders rejected has become the cornerstone" (Mark 12:10). If anyone understands feeling cast aside, Jesus does. And be assured, the One who broke rejection's very personal and crushing power when He rose from the dead will take you with Him out of rejection to new hope and life. To Jesus, helping you when you feel cast aside is personal, very personal.

WORDS FOR HEALING
Devotion Guide for Chapter Eight

READ 1 Samuel 2:1–10

REFLECT

These verses are Hannah's prayer after she presented Samuel to Eli in the temple. What triumph over rejection do you notice in Hannah's prayer?

What characteristics of God do you hear about in the prayer, and how do these qualities restore your confidence when you feel cast aside?

The final words of verse 9 say, "For not by might shall a man prevail." How does this encourage you in your weakness? How does a person prevail?

PRAY Hannah's prayer, adding specifics of your own struggle and thanking God for His faithful action on your behalf.

Thoughts
WHEN YOU THOUGHT YOUR LIFE
WOULD GO DIFFERENTLY

Then Daniel answered and said before the king, "Let your gifts be for yourself, and give your rewards to another. Nevertheless, I will read the writing to the king and make known to him the interpretation." (Daniel 5:17)

IT WASN'T SUPPOSED TO BE THIS WAY

Have you heard of Todd Marinovich? Todd was raised by his dad to be a sports prodigy—a football quarterback sensation, to be exact. Todd was fed healthy foods from the day he was born. He began to undergo physical conditioning by the time he reached his first birthday. He was given expert coaching and was schooled in every aspect of what it takes to become a professional football player. As a boy, he never ate a Big Mac or an Oreo cookie. His life was football, and his future was mapped out from his beginning.

But Todd's life didn't go as planned. After a successful high school football career, Marinovich received a football scholarship from the University of Southern California. While at USC, the drug use Todd began in high school became destructive and out of control. He bounced from college into the pros but left a path of trouble, conflict, and disappointment. Multiple arrests and stints in rehab punctuated his life. Instead of living the dream, his life was in shambles. Todd Marinovich thought his life would go differently. Everybody did. But life does not always turn out the way you expect. Sometimes, you're disappointed and hurt. On occasion—perhaps more often than you would have imagined—life twists and turns in a completely different way than you ever expected.

UNWELCOME SURPRISES

You may be going through just such a twist or turn at this very moment. Surprise! The worst news of your life just came your way.

Surprise! What was supposed to be a sweet season of existence has now become a time of your greatest grief and most terrifying fears. Surprise! What you thought would be a fulfilling phase of life is suddenly an experience that makes you sick to your stomach with worry and sorrow. You thought life would go differently. But the story you wrote in your mind and heart has been edited—rewritten—to contain everything that's all wrong.

It's a terrible feeling, but it's a common reality.

You may know Daniel, the boy from Jerusalem who became an unwilling prophet in Babylon. He understood the wrenching disappointment of a derailed life. Instead of enjoying a childhood with his family in his hometown, Daniel was led with fellow prisoners to a strange city where he was "volun-told" to serve the whims of an irrational ruler. But Daniel's unwelcome surprises may bring you important insight and direction for life that goes unpredictably wrong.

SHAPED BY FAITH

In Daniel 2, young Daniel was forced into panic mode. King Nebuchadnezzar had a bad dream. He was extremely troubled by his dream, but he couldn't remember it. So, he commanded his magicians, enchanters, and dream interpreters to tell him what he dreamed and what it meant. The king's advisers stood before him in disbelief. After trying to change the king's approach, the group said to him, "There is not a man on earth who can meet the king's demand. . . . The thing that the king asks is difficult, and no one can show it to the king except the gods, whose dwelling is not with flesh" (Daniel 2:10–11). So the king decided to execute all of his wise men—Daniel included. When word of the king's decree reached Daniel, he was sent scrambling. He asked the king for time. He went to his friends and asked them to join him in prayer. Throughout the night, they pleaded with God for an answer. And that night, in a vision from God, the mystery of the king's dream was revealed to Daniel. His unexpected ordeal brought about an unanticipated miracle.

When your life doesn't go the way you expect, you are put into the position of complete dependence on God. When everything comes crashing down, you can rush to despair or you can give God time. When unwelcome surprise hits, you can become despondent or you can rally friends to join you in prayer. When you have no idea what to do, you can let grief embitter you or you can watch for God's next step. God gave Daniel a gift he would have never seen in his former life. Only by traversing the unwanted road of his loss did Daniel's heart become shaped by faith. And at every turn, in each crisis, during every point of discomfort, God came through.

In Daniel 5, a new and even more unreasonable king took the throne. Daniel, now much older, was not even on the king's radar as someone who mattered. But that's when the king was frightened silly by a hand that appeared and wrote a mysterious message on the wall of his throne room. Daniel was summoned. Once again, this was not the life trajectory Daniel imagined. His path took a sharp left turn even in his captivity. At Daniel's lowest point of being forgotten and marginalized, God came through again. He gave Daniel courage to say to the king, who promised rewards and honor to the person who could interpret the handwriting on the wall, "Let your gifts be for yourself, and give your rewards to another. Nevertheless, I will read the writing to the king and make known to him the interpretation" (Daniel 5:17). Difficult moments may save you from meaningless distractions.

The next chapter of the Book of Daniel presents the best-known episode in Daniel's life: the time he was thrown into a den of lions. This was never one of his longed-for ambitions. But as the lions breathed down his neck, Daniel discovered something very important: God was with him. God was very close with a palpable presence to help and save him. It was a sweet treasure given in a sour situation.

Isn't that how it often goes? You may hate what life has handed you, but in those moments, you and everyone around you have a chance to witness the presence of your Savior and the dawn of hope.

Please allow me to add one more thought. Life's undesired turns underscore the importance of the gift of eternal life. The present has an irreplaceable purpose. God has an important reason for your existence this side of heaven. Life on earth can bring great blessing and joy. But your life now will never measure up to the eternity being prepared for you through the saving work of Jesus. Life may be going much differently than you had planned. But by faith and because of God's grace, your eternal life will never go wrong. God's presence in your pain is but a prelude to your eternal peace.

WORDS FOR HEALING
Devotion Guide for Chapter Nine

READ Psalm 43

REFLECT

What did the psalmist think God did?

What did the author of this psalm ask for?

Verse 5 is a refrain also used in Psalm 42. This seems to be a theme embedded by faith in the author's life. How does this refrain help you as you face life that has taken a wrong turn?

PRAY for God's hope and wisdom along the way of your journey. Ask God to show you His presence and direction as you venture into territory you never wanted.

Thoughts
WHEN YOU ARE FILLED WITH GUILT

And [Peter] went out and wept bitterly. (Luke 22:62)

THE VILLAIN

Snidely Whiplash was the name of the villain in the old Dudley Do-Right of the Mounties animated television segments that were part of *The Rocky and Bullwinkle Show*. Snidely was persistent in his persecution of the innocent waif, Nell Fenwick. Of course, Dudley and his faithful steed named "Horse" always came to the rescue. When I watched Dudley Do-Right, I never would have cast myself in the role of Snidely Whiplash. He was the bad guy. He did the wrong thing. I pictured myself as the hero, the good guy. I don't know of many people who would look at a villain and say, "That's what I want to be."

But like it or not, you can become a villain to people in your life. Thoughtless words cause injury. Irresponsible actions lead to heartbreak. Hurtful habits produce pain. Sometimes, you're just plain wrong. You do something bad. It's your fault. And because of what you've perpetrated, someone is hurt. Because of what you've done, damage lingers and will not fade.

Let's be honest. You're not always Dudley Do-Right. Sometimes, you're Snidely Whiplash. You're guilty of being a villain. God says it plainly: "All have sinned and fall short of the glory of God" (Romans 3:23); "If we say we have no sin, we deceive ourselves, and the truth is not in us" (1 John 1:8).

This is a hard pill to swallow. It's not easy to face your guilt head-on and say, "Yes, it's my fault. I was wrong." It would be much more pleasing to your ego to hear this: "Don't worry about it. What's done is done. Forget about it; move on. You're basically a good person. It's not your fault." But you know very well that those soothing words only mask a truth that can slowly and severely eat away at your soul.

You've done some things wrong. You've caused hurt. And you need to deal with that difficult and unsettling fact.

TRUTH AND FREEDOM

One thing I appreciate about God's Word is that it speaks with honesty—both brutal and healing. Instead of letting me live in denial, it tells me where I actually stand, what I need, and what God has done. It doesn't allow my guilt to fester and become toxic. It brings guilt out into the open so we can be freed from its heavy curse. If you remain connected to God's Word, Jesus said, "You will know the truth, and the truth will set you free" (John 8:32).

When you experience heartbreak, grief, and loss, guilt can be a huge and unspoken part of your pain. It may be too difficult to share. People may not know what to do with your confession of guilt: how you lashed out or were thoughtless when you saw your loved one for the last time, how you ruined a good thing because of your weakness and carelessness, how you brought the trouble on yourself, or how you replay in your mind and heart every regret you carry. But God doesn't make you live with hidden pain. He promises relief and forgiveness. Psalm 32:5 charts the course. The wrongdoing writer said to God, "I acknowledged my sin to You, and I did not cover my iniquity; I said, 'I will confess my transgressions to the LORD,' and You forgave the iniquity of my sin."

Freedom comes when the humbling risk of truth opens the way to forgiveness. Relief from guilt is realized only through honesty and vulnerability. That is the pathway God carves out through pain. The verses quoted above have important second halves. 1 John 1 says, "If we say we have no sin, we deceive ourselves, and the truth is not in us. If we confess our sins, [God] is faithful and just to forgive us our sins and to cleanse us from all unrighteousness" (vv. 8–10). Romans 3 tells us, "All have sinned and fall short of the glory of God, and are justified by His grace as a gift, through the redemption that is in Christ Jesus" (vv. 23–24). Acknowledging your sin before God doesn't cause condemnation—it reveals redemption. You can confess your guilt, your foul-ups, your carelessness, and your thoughtlessness to God. He will provide healing and relief from the burden that weighs you down. He will bring you freedom because Jesus takes your guilt away. King David said in Psalm 103, "As far as the east is from the west, so far does He remove our transgressions from us" (v. 12). The importance of the cross of Jesus Christ is underscored by the grievous pain of your guilt. Jesus suffered the consequences for your sin. Your debt is paid. In Christ, your guilt is removed.

LIVING IN FREEDOM

How do you now live with this good gift? Your sadness doesn't simply disappear in a moment. When do you start feeling better and less burdened?

The apostle Peter struggled with this question. After Jesus was arrested, Peter covertly followed Jesus' captors. As he spied out the proceedings against the Son of God, Peter was identified by some bystanders as one of Jesus' followers. Peter vehemently denied knowing Jesus. Three times, he disavowed his Master and Savior. Jesus had told him it would happen. "Before the rooster crows today," Jesus said to Peter, "You will deny Me three times" (Luke 22:61). When the rooster crowed that dark and difficult night, Peter's guilt rushed in. We're told that Peter "went out and wept bitterly" (v. 62).

But that wasn't the end of the story. After Jesus rose from the dead, He went looking for Peter. He pursued the guilt-ridden disciple. Finding him in his fishing boat, Jesus called Peter back to the beach for breakfast. Then three times, He asked Peter, "Do you love Me?" Three times, Peter answered, "Yes, Lord; You know that I love You." And three times, Jesus commissioned Peter to take care of His sheep, to follow Him, and to serve Him once again (John 21:4–19).

Jesus pursues you when you are guilty of being the villain. Time and time again, as you hear His Word and come into His presence, He will bring restoration and will release you from your guilt. He will commission you to follow Him and serve Him once again with a clear conscience and restored soul. Living in freedom takes time with Your Savior. Humbly and honestly listening to Jesus will empty your guilt of its power and set you free.

WORDS FOR HEALING
Devotion Guide for Chapter Ten

READ Psalm 103:1–14

REFLECT

What effect does God's forgiveness have according to verses 1–5?

Verses 8–10 make the character of God very clear. How is this good news for you today?

Verses 11–14 use powerful imagery to emphasize God's grace and mercy toward you. What in these verses do you need to hear most?

PRAY an honest prayer, confessing your guilt to God. Ask for His compassion and forgiveness in your weakness and sin. Thank Him for Jesus, who faithfully removed your sin as far as the east is from the west.

Thoughts

WHEN YOU KNOW LIFE ISN'T
SUPPOSED TO BE THIS WAY

The word of the LORD came to Abram in a vision: "Fear not, Abram, I am your shield; your reward shall be very great." But Abram said, "O Lord GOD, what will You give me, for I continue childless?" (Genesis 15:1–2)

PROMISES, PROMISES

Are you confused about what's happening in your life? Has an experience or a terrible disappointment left you heartbroken? You thought you knew how life would unfold. You were confident that you understood God's plan. But now, everything has gone haywire. Life isn't working the way it should. It isn't going according to what you thought the plan was. The unanticipated path you're on is frustrating, stressful, and filled with hurt. As you survey your current situation, you are certain that life isn't supposed to be this way.

You're not alone. That's exactly the trauma and confusion that gripped Abraham. God promised him, "I will make of you a great nation, and I will bless you" (Genesis 12:2). God gave Abraham the assurance: "Look toward heaven, and number the stars, if you are able to number them. So shall your offspring be" (Genesis 15:5). Those were wonderful promises from God. There was just one problem: Abraham and his wife, Sarah, had no children—and the clock was ticking. Abraham was seventy-five years old when God first promised him a bevy of descendants. He and his wife counted on God's promise. They waited and waited and waited some more. More than two decades of waiting went by and God kept promising. Then, when nearly a quarter of a century had passed, God appeared to Abraham again and repeated the assurance that he and Sarah would be the father and mother of many nations. How did Abraham respond? "Abraham fell on his face and laughed and said to himself, 'Shall a child be born to a man who is a hundred years old? Shall Sarah, who is ninety years old, bear a child?" (Genesis 17:17).

If your frustration wasn't so great and your sadness so deep, you might laugh too. But your pain and disappointment are no laughing matter. You know life is supposed to be better than this. You've heard the promise that God is loving and good, but in your grief and loss, that promise seems to be a lie. Why is God leaving you confused and disappointed? Why is loss being imposed on your life?

WAIT

Abraham couldn't figure it out. After God reiterated His promise of blessing, Abraham replied, "O Lord GOD, what will You give me, for I continue childless?" (Genesis 15:2). Then God brought Abraham outside on a crystal-clear evening and had him look at the sky. God said, "Look toward heaven, and number the stars, if you are able to number them. So shall your offspring be" (Genesis 15:5). What was Abraham's reaction? "He believed the LORD" (v. 6).

Abraham and Sarah believed God's promise, even though life bore no evidence of its fulfillment. They knew life was not supposed to be this way, but they trusted God to come through. The New Testament Book of Hebrews says, "By faith Sarah herself received power to conceive, even when she was past the age, since she considered Him faithful who had promised. Therefore from one man, and him as good as dead, were born descendants as many as the stars of heaven and as many as the innumerable grains of sand by the seashore" (Hebrews 11:11–12).

What do you do when you know life isn't supposed to be the way it is? You wait upon God. You consider Him faithful, and you wait. You believe in the One who promised instead of believing the outlook of the present. Psalm 27 underscores the calling to wait on God in faith: "I believe that I shall look upon the goodness of the LORD in the land of the living! Wait for the LORD; be strong, and let your heart take courage; wait for the LORD!" (vv. 13–14).

It's not easy to wait for God to come through. When life is crumbling around you and your disappointment and distress become overwhelming, you wonder if God is paying any attention at all. Abraham and Sarah wondered the same thing. After waiting for more than a decade, Abraham and Sarah took matters into their own hands. In order to make some progress, Abraham and Sarah agreed that he should have a child with Sarah's servant Hagar. Hagar became pregnant and gave birth to Abraham's son Ishmael, but no matter how much Abraham and Sarah plotted, planned, tried to implement plan B, or worked to force God's hand, God's timing and plan would unfold at His pace and in His time.

You may want to push God into action, convince Him to step up, or twist His arm to respond to your real and desperate needs. But God calls you to wait. Why? I don't know. Abraham and Sarah waited another thirteen years before their son, Isaac, was born. God wasn't toying with them or trying to make them squirm. He's not that way. As the great preacher and seasoned struggler Charles Haddon Spurgeon said, "God is too good to be unkind and He is too wise to be confused, and if I cannot trace His hand I can always trust His heart." When you are absolutely certain your life is not supposed to be the way it is, you can still trust God. You can still wait on Him.

Why? Because, as King David said in Psalm 27, "I shall look upon the goodness of the LORD in the land of the living" (v. 13). Because of Jesus, you have eternity as your ultimate hope and promise. Through His victory over disaster, brokenness, and death, your life has a new dimension—one that stretches beyond the circumstances of here and now. When you walk in faith, there is more to place your hope in than meets the eye. As you trust in God, you can wait on Him with confidence—even if it means waiting for eternity to be ushered in. Your Savior's death and resurrection made life what it is supposed to be. With His strength for today and His hope for tomorrow, you will not be disappointed.

Words for Healing
Devotion Guide for Chapter Eleven

READ Isaiah 40:25–31

REFLECT

Verses 25–28 remind you that God is up to any and every challenge in your life. How do these verses clarify your outlook and strengthen you in your doubts?

What restoration of your confidence in God do verses 29–31 give you?

What does it mean for you to wait on God during this season of your life, and what does God promise you as you wait?

PRAY for strength to wait on God, to put your hope in Him even though your present situation brings struggle. Thank your Savior for His understanding and His dependable help in your heartbreak.

Thoughts
WHEN YOU'RE DISAPPOINTED

And [Jesus] came to the disciples and found
them sleeping. (Matthew 26:40)

IT'S A BUST

Two doors down from my childhood home lived an inventor. No
fences separated the property in our little stretch of real estate, so
I had an unobstructed view into the yard of my eccentric and en-
trepreneurial neighbor. He was always tinkering with something,
wanting to make it big, hoping for a discovery that would change
the world. One year, a big orange trailer started to grow in his driveway. It began innocently enough. A black frame with wheels formed
the base. Then panels were attached to the frame. The contraption
was about the size of a small camping trailer. Mr. Inventor painted
the panels bright orange and spent months working covertly inside
the intriguing apparatus. One day, I came home from school and saw
words emblazoned on the side panels of the invention. This newly
developed revolutionary device was called the "Sno-Melter." We lived
in the Chicago area. My inventive neighbor was targeting the piles
of snow that accumulated in the city. He invented a snow-melting
machine!

It was a great concept. It could have changed snow-removal
methods forever. The Sno-Melter might have become one of the
most groundbreaking—or should I say, ice-eradicating—advances
in the frozen and blizzard-prone North. But it didn't. The invention
was a bust. I don't know why. It may not have been the right time.
Supporting technology may not have been available. Perhaps the
cost was prohibitive. My neighbor may not have known the right
people or just did not have the ability to sell the product. But the
Sno-Melter languished in his driveway, never realizing its intended
purpose. Instead of delightful success, my neighbor experienced
severe disappointment.

LETDOWNS

If you've ever tried something and failed, you know how my neighbor felt. You thought your strategy would do the trick. Your course of action seemed to be a good one. Your move made sense; your decision was sound. Seeing an opportunity, confronted with a need, or faced with a crisis, you made a plan. But somehow, the plan didn't work. You thought your life would turn out much better or that your loved one would benefit, but instead, you were left with disappointment—terrible and irreversible disappointment.

What do you do when that kind of heartbreak enters your life? You may feel angry. You may be laid low in hopelessness and discouragement. You may lash out in blame or withdraw in regret. Perhaps you feel like never again trying anything.

Jesus meets you in that place and fully understands how you feel. He had a plan for the evening before His crucifixion. Bringing His disciples to the Garden of Gethsemane, a peaceful refuge from the hubbub of the city, Jesus wanted to spend the night in prayer with His closest confidants and friends. He asked Peter, James, and John to accompany Him to a secluded area where they could ask for God's strength for their Master. Jesus began to agonize about what He faced. He said to the trio with Him, "My soul is very sorrowful, even to death; remain here, and watch with Me" (Matthew 26:38). So Jesus fell with His face to the ground and prayed, "My Father, if it be possible, let this cup pass from Me; nevertheless, not as I will, but as You will" (v. 39). This was an agonizing moment for Jesus. The Gospel writer Luke tells us that Jesus was praying with such intensity, His sweat fell to the ground like great drops of blood (Luke 22:44).

What were the disciples doing during this intense moment of need? How were Jesus' closest friends responding to His pain? They fell asleep. Not just once. Not twice. But three times! After being asked by Jesus for prayer support, after being begged by the Son of God to stick with Him, after being warned not to fall into temptation and fade in their spiritual devotion, these three disciples were a bust, a disappointment. Jesus' efforts and invitation, His plans and His hopes, led to a letdown in the Garden of Gethsemane. Even more, after investing three years of His life, love, and leadership in the band of twelve disciples, all of them failed Him. Judas betrayed Jesus; the other disciples fled. As you face your own disappointment, you can be assured that life didn't always work out for Jesus, either. He knows how your heartbreak feels.

RISE UP, PRESS ON

What can you do when you face disappointment? It's always a good idea to pay close attention to Jesus. What did He do after the letdown in the garden? He said to His disciples, "Rise, let us be going; see, My betrayer is at hand" (Matthew 26:46). Those are not expressions of dejection and despair. They are words of movement and mission, of power and purpose. During His darkest hour, Jesus pressed on to His ultimate destination. When your plans don't pan out the way you hoped, Jesus doesn't let you linger in despair. He says, "Rise up! Let's go! Onward!" His work of salvation is at hand. When your life seems like a bust, your Savior will bring you through. You don't need to dwell on disappointment. You don't need to blame someone or figure out why it happened. By God's grace and through the resurrection power of Jesus, you move forward in the life and calling He gives. You press on!

As the apostle Paul reflected on his losses, hardships, and disappointments, he said, "One thing I do: forgetting what lies behind and straining forward to what lies ahead, I press on toward the goal for the prize of the upward call of God in Christ Jesus" (Philippians 3:13–14). In disappointment, Paul was given a perspective of pressing on. It's what Jesus gives you when you face disappointment. Even though what you planned didn't work out, even though the hope you had in your heart didn't happen, Jesus lifts you up and brings you through the darkness. As you come face-to-face with deep disappointment, Jesus raises you up and sends you forward with His living Word. Add God's grace to any disappointment and you'll get hope, strength, and a future. Rise up, by faith in Jesus! With His grace, press on!

Words for Healing

Devotion Guide for Chapter Twelve

READ Psalm 20

REFLECT

How does this psalm speak truth even when you face disappointment?

How do verses 6–7 form a foundation for the previous verses and for your plans in life?

As you think about your disappointment and heartbreak, how has God's grace made verse 8 true for you?

PRAY this psalm—all the way to the final verse. Bring your hopes to God, telling Him why you will trust in Him no matter what happens. Thank Him for the ways He's caused you to "rise and stand upright."

Thoughts
WHEN YOU THOUGHT YOU WERE OVER IT

Then [Joseph] turned away from them and wept. (Genesis
42:24)

UNEXPECTED TEARS

Have you encountered unpleasant surprises of tears or gloom in
your grief journey? Just when you thought you were feeling well, sadness cast a dark shadow over your spirit. Right when you were convinced you could take up your normal routine, a debilitating sense of
dejection stopped you in your tracks. Has it happened to you too? Is
it happening now? At unexpected moments, your eyes well up with
tears. When you don't anticipate it, your heart becomes heavy and
your stomach feels dread. You tremble when you thought the trembling was over. You find a note. You hear a song. You feel the spring
breeze. You drive down a street. Someone tries to get in touch with
you. A date on the calendar comes around. You hear a child cry. You
go to a family gathering. And it all comes rushing back. You thought
you were over it, but the tears flow and the heartbreak hurts again.

You're not alone. Joseph endured thirteen years of heartbreak
before he was freed from prison and elevated to Pharaoh's sec-
ond-in-command. The young son of Jacob was thirty years old when
life finally came together. Over the next decade, Joseph seemed to
put his past pain behind him. He met and married a beautiful woman.
Together, they had two sons. Their children's names indicated that
Joseph had moved on from the turmoil, sadness, resentment, and
hurt of his past life. Genesis 41 tells us, "Joseph called the name of
the firstborn Manasseh. 'For,' he said, 'God has made me forget all
my hardship and all my father's house.' The name of the second he
called Ephraim, 'For God has made me fruitful in the land of my affliction'" (vv. 51–52). On the threshold of turning forty, Joseph was

confident that the past was in the past. It was gone. Joseph was over it—or so he thought.

After two years of worldwide famine, Joseph's brothers traveled to Egypt to buy some of the grain Joseph was stockpiling. The grain reserves were part of the famine protection plan Joseph had proposed to Pharaoh nine years before. When Joseph saw his brothers, the past came rushing back. He heard them whisper words of guilt and regret. He saw the expressions on their faces and was reminded of their cruelty. He remembered his own brashness and vanity. It was very strange. More than twenty years after Joseph was violently grieved by his brothers, after two decades of healing and forgetting, convinced that God made him forget his hardship and heartbreak, Joseph realized that grief does not easily disappear. It may recede into the background for a while, but the hurt remains real for a long time.

Do you ever wonder if your lingering hurt is abnormal? Ask Joseph. The strong and triumphant governor of Egypt with a new marriage, family, and identity had to turn away from his brothers as he began to weep over the pain he experienced years ago. You may think you're over it, but heartbreak has a habit of sticking around for the long haul.

WHY LOSS LINGERS

People may say to you about your grief, "Isn't it time you got over this? Isn't it time to move on?" But you know the truth. You can't "move on." You shouldn't "get over it." Not only do you need to work through your feelings, but you have a calling to dwell with your heartbreak and learn all you can from it. The very personal and difficult experience of grief will form your heart and shape your perspective. Sorrow may help open a pathway to depth and meaning you've never experienced before. Your anguish may increase your gratitude, your faith, your empathy, and your understanding.

Of course, grief should never become your taskmaster. It should also never send you into a life of denial. Heartbreak can never be given permission to steal the new days and opportunities God supplies. But you shouldn't waste what grief provides.

Joseph kept up his crying, but his tears told a story of personal growth and divine purpose. He wasn't over his ordeal of loss, but although the emotions surfaced inconveniently, Joseph realized some important truths about his life. He still loved his family. He had grown in humility. He had a new sense of gratitude and trust in God. So Joseph said to his brothers, "Do not be distressed or angry with yourselves because you sold me here, for God sent me before you to preserve life. . . . So it was not you who sent me here, but God" (Genesis 45:5, 8).

Joseph wept again when he asked his brothers to bring their father to Egypt. When he was reunited with his father after the long years of absence, we're told that Joseph threw his arms around his father's neck in a long embrace and sobbed for a long time (Genesis 46:29). Joseph wasn't "over it." He was growing because of it. After his father died, his brothers worried that Joseph was waiting until that moment to wreak revenge upon them. Joseph shed tears again and told them, "Do not fear, for am I in the place of God? As for you, you meant evil against me, but God meant it for good, to bring it about that many people should be kept alive, as they are today. So do not fear; I will provide for you and your little ones" (Genesis 50:19–21).

Joseph was fifty-six years old. The physical and emotional upheaval that broke his heart took place nearly forty years earlier. But the emotion still came rushing back. That's the way it goes with grief and heartbreak. When you think you're over it, the waves of emotion can sweep over you unexpectedly. But if humility before God and faith in His care are mingled with that emotion, you'll also see a new person whose heart, mind, and soul have been shaped by God's grace and steadfast love.

The apostle Paul said, "Blessed be the God and Father of our Lord Jesus Christ, the Father of mercies and God of all comfort, who comforts us in all our affliction, so that we may be able to comfort those who are in any affliction, with the comfort with which we ourselves are comforted by God" (2 Corinthians 1:3–4). God won't erase your past, but He will restore, rebuild, and reshape you in the present. Your Savior will use your heartbreak to grow you and to bless others.

WORDS FOR HEALING
Devotion Guide for Chapter Thirteen

READ Psalm 139:1–12

REFLECT

Verses 1–6 tell you that God knows you better than you know yourself. How does this help you when you feel heartbroken?

How do verses 7–10 give you comfort and encouragement in your journey of grief?

Verse 12 says that even darkness is not dark to God. How does this verse give you hope and strengthen you for the future?

PRAY about the darkness you feel. Tell God honestly what darkness covers you. Ask Him to stretch out His hand to protect you, to hold you, and to lead you into the future.

Thoughts
WHEN YOU DON'T THINK YOU'LL EVER BE HAPPY AGAIN

No, my daughters, for it is exceedingly bitter
to me for your sake that the hand of the LORD
has gone out against me. (Ruth 1:13)

WRECKAGE

Some observers speculated that the World Trade Center site in New York City would never be rebuilt after the 9/11 attacks. The devastation was so enormous, the grief was so profound, the shock was so severe, and the presence of loved ones' remains was so real that some people felt the site could never again be a place of bustling business.

Extreme destruction combined with emotional desolation can lead to feelings of enduring defeat. You may feel that way in your grief—like you will never be happy again.

A woman named Naomi found herself in that place. Cascading loss and heartbreak dominated Naomi's life. When famine swept over the land, she had to leave her hometown of Bethlehem with her husband and two sons. Uprooted and in survival mode, the family settled in a foreign and unfamiliar nation where making a living offered more promise. Just as the little group from Bethlehem began to put down roots, Naomi's beloved husband, Elimelech, died. Coping with heartbreak, she and her sons carried on with life. Her boys, Mahlon and Chilion, met local women, got married, and settled down. Life seemed to be smoothing out when, after ten years, both sons died. Why did grief keep invading Naomi's life? Without men to assert family rights and with no claim to property in the land of Moab, Naomi's only hope for safety and survival was to journey back to her hometown. Hearing that food was now more plentiful at home, she packed up her belongings and prepared to leave. First, however, she decided to have a heart-to-heart talk with her daughters-in-law. She said to them, "Go, return each of you to her mother's house. May the LORD deal kindly with you, as you have dealt with the dead and with me. The LORD grant that you may find rest, each of you in the house of her husband!" (Ruth 1:8–9).

But the young women did not want to go. They wept and replied, "No, we will return with you to your people" (v. 10). Naomi persisted. They would have no future with her, she told them. In all honesty, she felt that she would drag them down into pain and loss. She said, "No, my daughters, for it is exceedingly bitter to me for your sake that the hand of the LORD has gone out against me." Naomi was convinced that she would never again be happy. Her life was a shambles. All she wanted to do was disappear into her sadness.

RESURRECTION

You may feel the same way in your wreckage. How could you ever be happy again? The prospect of happiness seems ludicrous, too foolish to mention. You're devastated. You're filled with an enduring and serious sadness. Your loss has been catastrophic. Your heart will never be the same. You're in the exact same place as Naomi. You resonate with her words and can relate to her grief.

But if Naomi's story is your story, you may have a surprise in store. She would have never predicted the possibility of joy, but then her daughter-in-law Ruth spoke up. She told her bereaved and hopeless mother-in-law, "Do not urge me to leave you or to return from following you. For where you go I will go, and where you lodge I will lodge. Your people shall be my people, and your God my God. Where you die I will die, and there will I be buried. May the LORD do so to me and more also if anything but death parts me from you" (Ruth 1:16–17). God provided Naomi with someone who loved her and wanted to be with her. The lonely and lost woman now had loyal company. And there would be even more encouragement in store.

Ruth became Naomi's lifeline. A man in Bethlehem named Boaz fell in love with Ruth. Boaz happened to be a relative of Ruth's deceased husband. With love and care, Boaz stepped forward to serve as Ruth and Naomi's kinsman-redeemer, acquiring the rights and responsibility to the family land and to the widow Ruth and her family. In the place of loss, love blossomed. Instead of a future of sadness,

Naomi was blessed with surprising joy. And it got even better. Boaz married Ruth; then she conceived and gave birth to a baby boy. The women of Bethlehem said to the once-forsaken and bitter Naomi, "Blessed be the LORD, who has not left you this day without a redeemer, and may his name be renowned in Israel! He shall be to you a restorer of life and a nourisher of your old age, for your daughter-in-law who loves you, who is more to you than seven sons, has given birth to him" (Ruth 4:14–15). Naomi cradled the unexpected bundle of joy in her arms. They named the boy Obed. Grandma Naomi heard her friends declare, "A son has been born to Naomi." Obed was the heir Naomi could never have herself. From death came life. From bitterness came smiles. From hopelessness came happiness through God's provision.

This is your hope. The apostle Paul explained how this happens. Because of Jesus' death and resurrection, Paul said, "Death is swallowed up in victory" (1 Corinthians 15:54). Through Jesus Christ, the apostle noted, we're given that victory as a gift. In Jesus, new life has become your new normal. Because you have a Savior, there is hope for happiness even when you are convinced you'll never be happy again. Your caring and devoted God is the loyal company you need when life comes crashing down. The other bundle of joy born in Bethlehem, Jesus your Savior, brings you the surprising prospect of joy through His life, death, and resurrection.

Rising from the wreckage of ground zero in New York City is the Freedom Tower. Wrapped at its base by a beautiful memorial, the new structure pierces the clouds at 1,776 feet. Business bustles at the new 1 World Trade Center. And nobody forgets the loss that led to this resurrection.

A resurrection of joy awaits you. You don't have to fake it or force it to be your reality. You don't have to be happy right now or try to forget your grief. Patience and perseverance are prerequisites, but rising from the wreckage of your loss is the cross of Jesus Christ. Assuring your resurrection is the empty tomb of the Savior. At the right time, sooner or later, now or in eternity, your sadness will slip away and you will be surprised by new life—and the happiness that comes with it.

Words for Healing

Devotion Guide for Chapter Fourteen

READ Psalm 126

REFLECT

Verses 1–3 recount the homecoming of God's people after being held in captivity for generations. How does the reaction of the people in the psalm give you hope?

Verse 3 articulates the relationship between God's work and our joy. How do you see that relationship play out in your life?

How do verses 4–6 reflect your present reality and, at the same time, give you encouragement?

PRAY about your weeping and tears, letting God know why you are hurting. Ask Him to show you that you have hope for songs of joy.

Life
WHEN EVERYTHING CHANGES

At the end of the days I, Nebuchadnezzar, lifted
my eyes to heaven, and my reason returned to
me, and I blessed the Most High, and praised and
honored Him who lives forever. (Daniel 4:34)

CHANGES

One hundred years ago, life was very different. A friend of mine who was born in the early 1900s remembered being absolutely shocked when wealthy neighbors installed an indoor commode. At that time, when outhouses were the common location for restroom relief, she remembered thinking, How could they do *that* inside the house?

Changes in the past one hundred years have been dramatic, with the pace of change accelerating as each year passes. These days, technology is obsolete after only a couple of years. People expect newly developed innovation and design in shorter and shorter amounts of time. Rapid change has become normal—even longed for and embraced.

There's one exception, however. Nobody wants unwelcome change. You may be experiencing that right now. Life has undergone a dramatic shift. Your routines have been interrupted. You're missing formerly dependable conversations with people you cared about. Someone who was present and important to you is no longer in your life. Something very important is now absent. You feel lost, empty, incomplete, unnerved, and out of balance. This is not a change you wanted. It may not be a change you chose. It's an intrusion that turned your life upside down.

A KING'S LOSS

An ancient king walked the same road of uninvited change. His name was Nebuchadnezzar. We meet him as a mighty and confident conqueror in the first chapter of the Book of Daniel. But already in the second year of his reign, he began to experience a troubling shift in his life. Dreams began to plague him. Nebuchadnezzar was interested in spiritual things and searched for higher truths. But he couldn't understand the mysterious and vivid dreams that harassed him. His once certain and steady life now became a seesaw of instability. Nebuchadnezzar struggled to maintain his equilibrium. He worked hard to stay in control, but sweeping change overtook him. Twelve months after being warned about his arrogance, he strolled across the roof of his palace and exclaimed, "Is not this great Babylon, which I have built by my mighty power as a royal residence and for the glory of my majesty?" Immediately, his life was upended. We are told, "While the words were still in the king's mouth, there fell a voice from heaven, 'O King Nebuchadnezzar, to you it is spoken: The kingdom has departed from you, and you shall be driven from among men, and your dwelling shall be with the beasts of the field'" (Daniel 4:30–32).

King Nebuchadnezzar lost everything. From what the Bible tells us, the king seems to have been overtaken by insanity for seven years. The man who was in control lost control. The ruler who was revered by all roamed the fields like a wild animal. The dashing warrior feared by the nations descended into the life of a destitute wanderer. Daniel 4:33 tells us, "His body was wet with the dew of heaven till his hair grew as long as eagles' feathers, and his nails were like birds' claws." Nebuchadnezzar experienced devastating upheaval.

LIFT UP YOUR EYES

You may be able to relate to Nebuchadnezzar. Your life is not the same as it once was. Your loss is hard. Your new reality feels exhausting and bewildering. What can you do? How do you cope when unpleasant turmoil enters your existence?

The humbled king's life may provide help. Daniel warned the king that his loss would control his life until he acknowledged the preeminence of the God of heaven. In other words, the king couldn't work his way out of his own pain. The mighty ruler of Babylon didn't have the strength to control unwelcome change. Only God could help Nebuchadnezzar. Throughout the initial chapters of the Book of Daniel, we witness God's pursuit of Nebuchadnezzar. Over and over, God was working to create faith in the king's heart. Through Daniel, God miraculously revealed the meaning of the king's dreams. By rescuing Shadrach, Meshach, and Abednego from the fiery furnace, God showed Himself more powerful than the king's temper, authority, and executioners. Now, God wanted Nebuchadnezzar to receive the gift that brings dependable peace and eternal life: faith in Him. What was the king's only possible option when change rocked his world? He said, "I, Nebuchadnezzar, lifted my eyes to heaven, and my reason returned to me, and I blessed the Most High, and praised and honored Him who lives forever" (Daniel 4:34). When unwelcome change pulls you down, God calls you to lift your eyes to Him.

This is how God has led His precious children throughout the ages. Fully realizing that upheaval can be paralyzing, God has graciously provided access to His strength and salvation. The writer of Psalm 121 reflected the sentiment of King Nebuchadnezzar. The psalmist affirmed, "I lift up my eyes to the hills. From where does my help come? My help comes from the LORD, who made heaven and earth" (vv. 1–2).

What do you do when your life is in total upheaval? Lift up your eyes to your Savior. Look to the One who can rescue and strengthen you. Let the One who made His way through the havoc of sin and death chart your course through unwelcome change. Ask Jesus to lead the way from moment to moment, step-by-step.

The last word we hear from Nebuchadnezzar is one of devoted dependence on the God who saves. The king declared, "Now I, Nebuchadnezzar, praise and extol and honor the King of heaven, for all His works are right and His ways are just; and those who walk in pride He is able to humble" (Daniel 4:37). When change arrived, the humbled king found his refuge in the One who is changeless. You have the same source of strength in your disorder: "Jesus Christ is the same yesterday and today and forever" (Hebrews 13:8). He will walk with you and hold you steady through every painful change.

WORDS FOR HEALING

Devotion Guide for Chapter Fifteen

READ Psalm 121

REFLECT

How do verses 1–4 guide you when your life is in painful upheaval?

Verses 5–8 give you powerful promises. What consolation do you receive from these verses even when God doesn't seem close to you?

How might prayer be a tool that can replace sadness, frustration, or worry in your life?

PRAY about the changes that grieve your heart. Lift up your eyes to your Savior and ask Him to help you in your time of need. Thank Him for never abandoning you and for providing eternal hope.

Life
WHEN YOU CAN'T DO WHAT YOU USED TO

Moses fled from Pharaoh and stayed in
the land of Midian. (Exodus 2:15)

SIDELINED

Do you feel frustrated that you can't do what you used to do? At
one time, you fit in and were fit for the task at hand. You were strong
and steady, respected and ready. You were keenly focused on your
purpose and welcomed at the table by all. But now, everything has
changed. You aren't able to tackle what you once did so well. Doors
have closed. Opportunities have become limited. Friends have drifted away. You're not the go-to person anymore.

You can still accomplish a lot. You've got know-how and desire.
Your experience is top tier. But you're not in the loop. Things aren't
the same as they used to be. It feels like you're in a wilderness, as if
you're a stranger separated from times that felt familiar and friendly.
These days, you question your own identity and worth. You've lost a
central part of your being, and that loss has left you uncertain, inse-
cure, and in limbo.

It's a terrible feeling to be sidelined. What do you do when your
"sweet spot" is suddenly gone? A man named Moses may offer an
answer. Moses barely survived his childhood. Born as a Hebrew boy
in Egypt, he and his fellow Israelites became a threat to Pharaoh, the
Egyptian ruler. Fearful that the Hebrew people would overtake the
Egyptians in strength and numbers, Pharaoh gave a fearsome decree.
He ordered his people, "Every son that is born to the Hebrews you
shall cast into the Nile" (Exodus 1:22). The cruel and callous order
put thousands of lives in jeopardy, including baby Moses. But Moses'
mother would not capitulate to the evil Egyptian king. After hiding
her son at home for three months, she coated a basket with tar,
placed her infant inside, and hid the basket in the reeds along the
bank of the Nile River. Moses' sister Miriam watched from a distance

to see what would happen to her floating baby brother.

Instead of being lost in the river, Moses was found by Pharaoh's daughter. As she opened the basket and saw the crying Hebrew baby, her heart went out to him. She wanted this little one as her own. Unknowingly enlisting the help of Moses' mother, Pharaoh's daughter named the infant Moses and adopted him as a prince of Egypt. Moses lived a charmed life until he was about forty years old. That's when he saw the violent abuse of one of his fellow Hebrews by an Egyptian taskmaster. Moses reacted with thoughtless fury. Thinking there were no witnesses nearby, Moses killed the Egyptian. But someone saw his crime, Moses' cover was blown, and Pharaoh sought his life. Filled with fear, Moses fled to the distant wilderness land of Midian.

There, Moses realized he was sidelined. He couldn't do what he once did and was unable to pursue what he wanted to accomplish. He was no longer welcome at the palace, and his people wouldn't accept him as a deliverer. Moses settled down in Midian, took up the lowly occupation of sheepherding, and lay low in discouragement. After his marriage and the birth of his son, Moses gave an indication about how he felt. He named his son Gershom, meaning "a stranger there." The former prince and aspiring deliverer languished in limbo for forty years.

STUCK?

You may feel like you're stuck in uselessness right now. It may be self-imposed like Moses, or your futility may have been forced on you because of unfair and unfortunate circumstances. Perhaps the passage of time has taken you out of circulation. However it's happened, being forcefully removed from what you are passionate about is a hard and hope-draining burden. Passing time doing what seems worthless is not only no fun, but it also drains your self-esteem, makes you feel like a failure, and causes you to wonder if you have any future. If too much time drags on with no change and no possibilities, you may feel yourself sliding into a numbing and hopeless despair. What can you do when you feel absolutely powerless?

You may not be able to do anything, but God can. When you can't do what you used to, God still does what He does best. He hears you, He comes to you, He saves you, and He sends you. He underscores your dignity and worth. Even when you find yourself in unfamiliar territory, God still knows where you are and has an important purpose for you. Remember, you may feel as if your best days are past, but God may be preparing you for your most significant mission. You may not be able to do what you used to, but your new mission may be where God wants you.

SENT

Just ask Moses. His first forty years in the wilderness as a shepherd prepared him for his next forty years in the wilderness as a deliverer. In what he thought was the twilight of his life, eighty-year-old Moses was recruited by God for a new mission. Meeting him in the wilderness, God told him, "I have surely seen the affliction of My people who are in Egypt and have heard their cry because of their taskmasters. I know their sufferings, and I have come down to deliver them out of the hand of the Egyptians and to bring them up out of that land to a good and broad land. . . . Come, I will send you to Pharaoh that you may bring My people, the children of Israel, out of Egypt" (Exodus 3:7–8, 10). Moses was given new marching orders. He never would have scripted his life that way, but Moses became the man who led the people of Israel out of Egypt. With miraculous signs and wonders, Moses convinced Pharaoh to give the Hebrews freedom. Moses raised his staff to part the waters of the Red Sea. Everyone witnessed the power of God that miraculous day. Moses met with God on Mount Sinai to receive the Ten Commandments. Through twists, turns, and adventure, Moses guided the Israelites to the Promised Land. It was said about him: "There has not arisen a prophet since in Israel like Moses, whom the LORD knew face to face" (Deuteronomy 34:10).

What did Moses learn? God never forgets about you. He waits for you. In His grace, He sustains you. He sends you to do His work in the right places at the right time. God knows what He is doing. Sometimes, when you feel like a misfit, you need to let go of what you knew in the past and let God show you His kindness and purpose in the present. Be assured that when you can't do what you used to, Jesus stands with you. Your purpose will always be found in His presence.

Words for Healing
Devotion Guide for Chapter Sixteen

READ Psalm 13

REFLECT

The first two verses of Psalm 13 ask challenging questions. What similar questions do you have for God in your heartbreak?

In verses 3–4, King David, the author of this psalm, saw a bigger picture of his frustration. If you feel like you're in limbo, what do you believe is at stake beyond your personal feelings and needs?

How do verses 5–6 challenge you, reassure you, and guide you?

PRAY a prayer of faith and trust in the steadfast love of God. Thank Him for ways He is showing His faithfulness and goodness as you wait for Him to act.

Life
WHEN YOU HAVE A GOOD DAY—AND FEEL GUILTY

Simon Peter, Thomas (called the Twin), Nathanael
of Cana in Galilee, the sons of Zebedee, and two
others of His disciples were together. Simon Peter
said to them, "I am going fishing." They said to
him, "We will go with you." (John 21:2–3)

THE WEIGHT OF THE WORLD

On your journey through heartbreak, has a good day surprised
you? You found yourself laughing, enjoying something you love, or
feeling lighthearted. You felt as if the day was normal. But how could
that be? How could you be happy at a time like this? Will people
think you don't care? Are you forgetting the importance of your loss?
Why should you be able to enjoy life again? Is it right to feel normal?

When you experience loss and sadness, you may be tempted to
believe that you have to carry the weight of all the trouble in your life.
If *you* don't take it seriously, give it attention, process it, and shoulder it, who will? After all, you want to honor your loss and be healthy
with your feelings. You don't want to veer into denial. You don't want
to forget the lessons you're learning or act as if the gravity of your
grief doesn't matter. So you take the heavy load and lug it with you
from morning till night.

But I wonder if you're forgetting Jesus' gracious invitation for
people who bear burdens. He said, "Come to Me, all who labor and
are heavy laden, and I will give you rest. Take My yoke upon you,
and learn from Me, for I am gentle and lowly in heart, and you will
find rest for your souls. For My yoke is easy, and My burden is light"
(Matthew 11:28–30).

It's important for you to understand a vital fact about your
heartbreak. Yes, your loss is serious. It is weighty and difficult. It is
real and will never stop being a part of your life. But you are not the
primary carrier of this burden—Jesus is. Because of His care for you,

you can have some time off. By His grace, you can get some rest. Let the cross of Christ convince you that the weight of the world is not yours to carry.

FISHING WITHOUT CRITICISM

After the apostle Peter denied knowing Jesus, and after Jesus' brutal death and victorious resurrection from the dead, Peter felt the sting of his betrayal. In Jesus' two initial appearances to His disciples after His resurrection, Peter was overjoyed to see his Savior alive. But the burdened follower of the Messiah wondered if he was of any use to his Lord. One day, perhaps seeking some normalcy, Peter said to his fellow fishermen, "I am going fishing." A group of six accompanied him to the Sea of Galilee for an evening expedition. Fishing is what Peter knew. He felt comfortable in the boat and on the sea. Fishing may have been Peter's safe haven, the place he could ponder the complexities of life, see the wonder of creation, and rejoice in the sights, smells, and sounds of his childhood. For Peter, a day that included fishing was probably a very good day. John 21 says that the group of seven didn't catch anything that night, but it probably didn't matter. Peter was in his element. Life felt normal. His heartbreak was on hold for a little while. The group of men probably conversed, joked, and enjoyed the evening.

As the sun began to rise, Jesus stood on the shore. He was searching for Peter and his companions and watched them as they finished their fishing efforts. Then Jesus called out to them. What did He say to the group? What message did the risen Savior have for the men in the boat that morning? Did He chastise them for forsaking God's mission? Did He scold them for wasting time? Did Jesus remind them that they blew it a few days earlier and shouldn't be having fun at a serious time like this? No, Jesus called out to them and asked if they had caught anything. Hearing the reply that their expedition was a bust, He directed them, "Cast the net on the right side of the boat, and you will find some" (John 21:6). The disciples threw the net as directed and, to their absolute amazement, caught 153 large fish in one cast. There were so many fish in the net that they couldn't haul it into the boat.

Jesus didn't squelch His disciples' happiness; He increased it. He didn't put a damper on Peter's good day; He put an exclamation point on it. Jesus doesn't wince at the prospect of experiencing joy in the midst of heartbreak and loss; He revels in it.

THE LORD IS GOOD

What happened next? The disciples recognized it was Jesus who was speaking to them. They hurried to the shore and gathered around the risen Son of God. Was it now time to dispense with the pleasantries and get down to the business of betrayal and hurt? Did Jesus glare at the grown men and give them a talking-to? No, Jesus said to the bewildered fishermen, "Come and have breakfast" (John 21:12).

You see a trend here, don't you? The gladness Jesus provides isn't held captive by your grief. In Him, because of Him, you can have a good day. You can rejoice. You can rest from your weariness and loss. The apostle Paul captured this strange but soul-restoring dynamic when he said, "We rejoice in our sufferings, knowing that suffering produces endurance, and endurance produces character, and character produces hope" (Romans 5:3–4).

When you have a good day, God's hope is coming to the surface. His goodness and grace are prevailing in your life. Your good day gives evidence to the fact that you're not in charge of the universe. You can have a day off from your grief because your Comforter is always on the job. Jesus said, "In the world you will have tribulation. But take heart; I have overcome the world" (John 16:33). That's how Jesus can sneak some joy into your life when you least expect it. That is why you can enjoy a good day and not feel guilty at all. Your happiness is a gracious gift of rest and relief from the giver of all good things.

WORDS FOR HEALING
Devotion Guide for Chapter Seventeen

READ Psalm 136

REFLECT

A refrain occurs in every verse of this psalm. How does this repeating phrase reinforce your faith in God's character and in His attitude toward you?

Verses 1–9 talk about creation, and verses 10–22 recall God's saving work for the people of Israel. How do you relate to the joy and happiness seen in these great deeds?

The final verses of the psalm get very personal. How do these verses describe God's goodness in your life?

PRAY Psalm 136, inserting your reasons to give thanks to God, adding the refrain of "His steadfast love endures forever" to each of your items of gratitude.

Life

WHEN YOU WANT TO GO BACK TO THE WAY IT WAS

The whole congregation of the people of Israel grumbled
against Moses and Aaron in the wilderness. (Exodus 16:2)

LOOKING BACK

Were your "good old days" some of your best days? When you
look back, do times past contain some of your most beautiful moments and treasured memories? It may be that, before everything
changed, you were enjoying some of the best times of your life. It was
your heyday. It was when your dreams came true. It was when you
looked forward to waking up in the morning. Those days were filled
with love and laughter. You enjoyed meaningful conversations and
good company. You felt like you were in your sweet spot. Of course,
you faced challenges now and then, but even when difficulties hit,
your heart felt full and all was well. Back then, during that time, your
life was filled with good things.

But now, it's a different story. A big part of your former happiness is missing. Change has swept in—and it's not for the better. You
don't meet mornings with enthusiasm. You face nights with dread.
The days have an emptiness about them. Your heart feels hollow. You
wonder why it can't be like it once was. You yearn for good times past.
Why can't you go back?

IS IT OKAY TO YEARN?

When you face loss, it is normal to pine for the past. During hard
times and in the midst of new challenges, you may find yourself wish-
ing it could be the way it once was. Even when previous times were
difficult, the familiar is sometimes more comfortable than the new.
After God's people were freed from slavery in Egypt, their new uncertainty caused them to long for their previous life in Egypt. As soon
as the group landed in the wilderness, their complaints began: "The
whole congregation of the people of Israel grumbled against Moses

and Aaron in the wilderness, and the people of Israel said to them, 'Would that we had died by the hand of the LORD in the land of Egypt, when we sat by the meat pots and ate bread to the full, for you have brought us out into this wilderness to kill this whole assembly with hunger' " (Exodus 16:2–3).

The people were starving, scared, and sleep deprived. They were in a situation they had never faced before. Familiar routines and feelings of security were gone. What they had known for generations was now topsy-turvy. Was it wrong for them to want to go back to the way it was? It's a question you may wonder about. Will you be like Lot's wife if you look back? She yearned for her old city of Sodom, and with one glance back toward her previous life, she turned into a pillar of salt. When you long for the days before your loss, are you being unfaithful and wasteful? In this new season of life, are you supposed to buck up, keep a stiff upper lip, and forge ahead?

God's response to the grumbling of the people in the wilderness may surprise you and may give you an encouraging answer when you feel like you want to go back to the way it was. After the people voiced their complaint, God said to Moses, "I have heard the grumbling of the people of Israel. Say to them, 'At twilight you shall eat meat, and in the morning you shall be filled with bread. Then you shall know that I am the LORD your God' " (Exodus 16:11–12).

Did you notice God's reply to the group of complaining and rearward-looking people? He didn't turn anyone into a pillar of salt. He spoke no words of condemnation. He didn't shake them by their collars and tell them to toughen up, get over it, and get with the program. What did God do? He blessed them and provided for them so they could know Him as they traveled on their new journey.

BLESSED

God does the same for you as you look back fondly at the past. He doesn't tell you to forget the good times of your former life. He doesn't demand that you separate yourself from treasured memories and precious moments. No, He understands your yearning and responds with blessing and provision right now. God sent quail into the people's camp so they could have meat to eat. He also provided manna, the sweet, breadlike wafer that covered the ground and nourished the travelers during their time in the wilderness. He answered their craving with tender care. He reminded the people that they weren't walking through the wilderness without a purpose; they were walking toward a new land with new promise.

God blesses you with that beautiful certainty and gentle care. He provides His Word to nourish and encourage you. He blesses you with people who show love and understanding. He doesn't rush you on your journey but takes each step with you. And He provides important reassurance in your wilderness: by God's grace, you are walking through your pain toward a promise. By faith, with your Savior as your companion, you are traveling in God's care, heading into His new plan for your life and, ultimately, to the gift of eternal peace and fulfillment. You may want to go back to the old days, but God has some new days planned that will delight you.

As you travel through your wilderness, it's okay to look back. You can remember and reminisce. You can treasure the good gifts of the past, being confident that God will bless you and provide for you in the present. Even more than His provision, however, you are blessed with God's presence. He wants you to know Him. When good times fill your life, you can see and be grateful for God's goodness, but when difficult times overtake you, you need to know the nearness of your Savior. God voiced His primary goal for His wilderness-wandering people. He said, "Then you shall know that I am the LORD your God." This is an intimate and personal statement. God wanted to show this troubled and worried group that He was dependable in His devotion to them, He was powerful to protect them, and He was a close companion who would always care for them.

That is God's message for you as you make your way into a new and unfamiliar future. You can look back. You can yearn for former days. You can remember treasured times. But as you do, you can always be certain that in your travels to new territory, God is dependable in His devotion to you, powerful to protect you, and your close companion who will always care for you.

WORDS FOR HEALING
Devotion Guide for Chapter Eighteen

READ Psalm 145

REFLECT

Verses 1–7 sing praise to God for His faithfulness and goodness throughout generations. For what blessings of your past are you most thankful?

As you read verses 8–13, you hear of God's gracious work in the present. How do you see God's grace and provision in your present situation?

The psalm closes with promises for the future. What comfort, encouragement, and reassurance do verses 14–21 give you?

PRAY a prayer of thanksgiving for the blessings of the past. Let God know your concerns about the present and the future. Share with Him how His promises strengthen and comfort you.

Life
WHEN YOUR DREAM DIES

[God said to Abraham,] "Take your son, your only son Isaac, whom you love, and go to the land of Moriah, and offer him there as a burnt offering on one of the mountains of which I shall tell you." (Genesis 22:2)

YOUR DREAM

Has your dream died? Your dream may have been a worthy and wonderful scenario for yourself or someone you love, but now the likelihood of that possibility is gone. You may have had great hope that your life would turn out a certain way, but now that hope has disappeared. You had a picture of the future. It wasn't unreasonable or over the top. It was good and honorable and even God pleasing. It made sense. But for some unknown and mystifying reason, that dream is not going to become a reality. Your hope is not going to happen. You thought you were on the way. It appeared that all was well. But what you imagined life would look like is now lost. Your reality has twisted and turned into total tumult and disappointment.

This is a crushing and confusing blow. It is gut-wrenching to come to grips with this kind of grief. When you invest your life in worthy hope, a senseless setback is heartbreaking. This disheartening scenario is what played out in the life of Phil Vischer. Vischer is the creative personality who developed the animated video series *Veggie Tales*. The vegetable characters that told Bible stories became a hit. Millions of videos were sold. The popularity of *Veggie Tales* led to the formation of Vischer's company, Big Idea Productions. In its heyday, more than two hundred employees swarmed the Chicago-area campus, helping to produce Bible videos that brought God's message of grace to children and adults. It was Phil's dream to make a difference for Christ.

But then, the bottom dropped out. Sales plateaued. A key project turned out to be a disappointment. A lawsuit that seemed as if it wouldn't prevail resulted in a multimillion-dollar verdict against Phil's company. That disastrous decision led to layoffs and bankruptcy. Phil wondered how something doing so much good could be allowed to fall apart.

You may be wondering the same thing.

ABRAHAM'S DREAM

Abraham and Sarah dreamed that one day they would have a child. God fueled that dream by promising the couple many descendants who would bring blessing to the world. But as Abraham approached one hundred years of age and Sarah hit ninety, the prospect of a bouncing baby boy looked very dim. That's when God stepped in with a miracle. He made the dream come alive by blessing the over-the-hill couple with their son, Isaac. Can you imagine the delight, the joy, and the celebration resulting from the birth of this baby? Can you envision the love Abraham and Sarah felt toward this precious little gift in their lives—their dream come true?

But after Isaac was old enough to walk, talk, and do chores, God approached Abraham with a strange and surprising command. God said, "Take your son, your only son Isaac, whom you love, and go to the land of Moriah, and offer him there as a burnt offering on one of the mountains of which I shall tell you."

What was going on here? The false gods of foreign nations demanded this kind of burnt offering. The thoughtless and cruel religions of other countries treated life cheaply and lived selfishly. But the true God, the God who spoke personally and promised blessing, the God who did miracles and showed mercy to those who were vulnerable, the God of grace and compassion—what was He asking? What was He doing to their dream?

How did Abraham respond? "So Abraham rose early in the morning, saddled his donkey, and took two of his young men with him, and his son Isaac. And he cut the wood for the burnt offering and arose and went to the place of which God had told him" (Genesis 22:3). As Phil Vischer agonized over the death of his dream, he reflected on people like Abraham. Years ago, I heard Vischer say, "When the people of great faith in the Bible didn't know what to do, they didn't do anything. They waited on God."

That was Abraham's course of action when faced with the death of his dream. He didn't believe his God was like the other gods. He trusted that God had a gracious and wonderful plan for him and for the world. He was certain the plan involved his son, Isaac. But instead of protesting, trying to correct God, disobeying God's command, or taking matters into his own hands, Abraham did nothing. He went, and he waited on God. God's Word explains Abraham's faith: "By faith Abraham, when he was tested, offered up Isaac. . . . He considered that God was able even to raise him from the dead" (Hebrews 11:17, 19). Abraham knew that the true God, the God of heaven, the living God of compassion and grace, was better than the way things seemed.

LIVING BY FAITH

This is the truth you can trust when your dream dies. You don't have to descend into hopelessness; you can depend on the One who raises the dead. The writer of the Book of Hebrews said that, figuratively speaking, God *did* bring Isaac back from death. You may remember that just as Abraham lifted a knife to slay his beloved offspring, the angel of the Lord called out to Abraham from heaven, "Abraham, Abraham! Do not lay your hand on the boy or do anything to him" (Genesis 22:11–12). Then Abraham looked and saw a ram caught in a bush. This provision from God was a substitute to take the place of Isaac. A relieved Abraham named that place "The LORD will provide" (v. 14).

You may say, "Well, Abraham got his dream back." You're right. But just because we know the end of Abraham's odyssey, we cannot discredit his heartbreak and suffering during the ordeal. You may be in the midst of your suffering, but you also walk with the God who raises the dead. You have a Savior who became a substitute for you when He was slain on the cross. God provides for you, and He will come through. It may be sooner. It may be at the very last moment when all looks lost. It may be much later. But you walk with the God of Abraham. Abraham's son, Isaac, and God's beloved Son, Jesus, are proof that God's good dreams for you will prevail. Take heart and wait on Him.

WORDS FOR HEALING
Devotion Guide for Chapter Nineteen

READ Lamentations 3:13–26

REFLECT

The Book of Lamentations is a record of the brokenhearted prophet Jeremiah's outcries after the destruction of Jerusalem and its people. How do verses 13–20 reflect your own suffering and sadness?

Verses 21–24 introduce hope in the middle of what seemed completely hopeless. How do these verses help you?

How do the promise and action of verses 25–26 strengthen you during your struggle?

PRAY that God comes through in His gracious way and at His right time as you face your loss and heartbreak. Let Him know what you need, and ask Him to show you His great faithfulness today.

Life

WHEN YOUR GIFTS SEEM WASTED

[God said to Jeremiah,] "See, I have set you this day over nations and over kingdoms, to pluck up and to break down, to destroy and to overthrow, to build and to plant." (Jeremiah 1:10)

AN UNEXPECTED LIFE

You have so much to give. You possess unique talents and abilities. You are passionate about important and exciting areas of life that can impact people positively and powerfully. But you're not being given a chance—or the possibilities are being pulled away from you. At every turn, you seem to be going backward instead of forward. People who don't have half of your desire or drive are receiving the opportunities you crave. But you languish as an underutilized misfit. Are you trapped in the disappointment of wondering why you can't do what you were created to accomplish?

You just want a chance, an opportunity, an open door. Why does it seem that all the doors close in your face? Why is your heart's desire left unfulfilled and ignored? Why must you travel a path you never wanted?

Jeremiah, a powerful prophet in the Old Testament, was a priest's son who was groomed and educated to follow in the footsteps of his father. He had a promising future, serving the people of Judah as they offered their sacrifices to God and acting as a focal point of faith and life for the community. There was just one problem: the people of the community had become hypocritical and two-faced. They were living selfish and loveless lives, while spouting lofty spiritual platitudes. They trampled on the poor and weak, gave their lives to false gods, and turned from truth and goodness. This was a corrupt and chaotic time, and it completely changed Jeremiah's future. Instead of using his education and gifts to serve as a priest, Jeremiah was commissioned by God as a prophet. Jeremiah was chosen to speak the plain and unvarnished truth of God to a rebellious people.

This is not something Jeremiah had asked for. Instead of living a fulfilling life of service, his day-to-day existence became filled with trouble, criticism, persecution, frustration, and pain. He started his prophetic work as an unseasoned youth and endured what seemed like a fruitless task until the day he died as a weary old man in exile. He uttered statements like: "O LORD, You have deceived me, and I was deceived; You are stronger than I, and You have prevailed. I have become a laughingstock all the day; everyone mocks me" (Jeremiah 20:7).

Jeremiah is known as "the weeping prophet." You may feel the same way. You may be wondering why your life, with plenty of eager ability and energy, is being squandered. Why are your gifts being wasted? Why can't you do what you want to do? Why must you endure a heartbreaking and unwanted trek through life?

WORDS FOR AN UNWANTED JOURNEY

But Jeremiah didn't receive only an unfulfilling task. He was also given a reassuring promise. Jeremiah recounted the episode: "Now the word of the LORD came to me, saying, 'Before I formed you in the womb I knew you, and before you were born I consecrated you; I appointed you a prophet to the nations.' Then I said, 'Ah, Lord GOD! Behold, I do not know how to speak, for I am only a youth.' But the LORD said to me, 'Do not say, "I am only a youth"; for to all to whom I send you, you shall go, and whatever I command you, you shall speak. Do not be afraid of them, for I am with you to deliver you, declares the LORD' " (Jeremiah 1:4–8).

God promised to be with Jeremiah. That powerful promise takes place throughout God's Word. For every challenge, in every unwanted assignment, through self-doubt and uncertainty, God promises you His presence. One of Jesus' final statements before He ascended into heaven was this: "I am with you always, to the end of the age" (Matthew 28:20). The greatest meaning in your life may not be in what you do, but in how Jesus meets you where you are. Jeremiah knew God needed him to serve in a thankless and heartbreaking role. But he was confident God would never abandon him on the arduous journey.

You may feel like your place in life is a waste of your gifts, but that precise place may be where God needs what you can uniquely give. Your unwanted journey may be God's most urgent mission. That's why you need God's presence every step of the way. Even for unwanted journeys—perhaps especially for them—God gives His living Word to nourish you and His presence in Holy Communion to renew you. He is with you to encourage you, strengthen you, and help you.

MORE THAN MEETS THE EYE

A quick glance at Jeremiah's life may cause people to shake their heads and say, "What a waste." After all, the Book of Jeremiah displays the prophet's exceptional talent and character. His message is authentic, deep, and penetrating. Jeremiah's heart is passionate, and his prophecies are filled with insight. But he didn't seem to make any difference. The people didn't listen. They even tried to kill him. He ended up running for his life and seeing his beloved nation overrun by violent and pagan warriors.

But a closer look and a longer view bring a different assessment. More than six hundred years after they were written, Jeremiah's words were still being quoted by New Testament writers. One of the most well-known and encouraging verses of the Bible is from Jeremiah's writings. The verse is posted on a large plaque hanging above the front door of my home. It says,

> "For I know the plans I have for you," declares the LORD,
>
> "plans to prosper you and not to harm you,
>
> plans to give you hope and a future."
>
> Jeremiah 29:11 (NIV)

I doubt that Jeremiah ever imagined any of his words having such an impact on so many people for so long a time. But God never wastes a life. He will not waste *your* life. What you may perceive as a mishap and mistake may in reality be one of God's great works of majesty and grace. You can take heart when you feel like your gifts are being wasted. God is with you, and He is making His difference through you—even at this very moment.

Words for Healing

Devotion Guide for Chapter Twenty

READ Jeremiah 31:1–6, 16–17

REFLECT

The Book of Jeremiah gives surprising and heart-restoring hope. How do you think verses 1–6 encouraged the people who saw their lives disintegrating before them?

How do these verses restore your hope when you feel as though your gifts are being wasted?

How do verses 16–17 help you cope when you feel as though you're not doing what you want to do in your life?

PRAY a prayer of thanksgiving for God's presence. Let God know how you've seen Him show up in your life and what hopes you have for the future. Ask Him to be with you no matter what happens.

Life

WHEN REALITY HITS HOME

Nathan said to David, "You are the man!" (2 Samuel 12:7)

REALITY

When a friend of mine saw a beautiful sunset over the lake behind her home, she was hit with the powerful realization that everything had changed. Memories and sadness came rushing in. Her loss became very real. For another friend, it was the financial disaster that enveloped her. She was no longer able to support her family, and the reality of being alone became an unwelcome reality. For you, it may be something completely different: a date on the calendar comes around; a holiday celebration takes place; a smell, a taste, a sound, or a song brings everything back; a person reminds you of how real your heartbreak is.

You never know when loss will become a reality. Oftentimes, after heartbreak hits, you put your head down and plow ahead. You take care of what's urgent, attend to details, keep busy, and move ahead with life. But moments will come—unexpectedly and suddenly—when your hurt becomes real. The lasting nature of your loss stands before you clearly and unrelentingly. It may be when quiet descends into your life for a moment or two. Or it may catch you by surprise when you thought you were doing really well.

No matter how it happens, when reality hits home, you may feel like the wind has been knocked out of you. The finality of your grief blankets you like a thick and heavy fog. You may feel lost.

GOD STEPS IN

In those moments of stark reality, you need to hear another important reality: Jesus, the very Son of God who came to dwell with you as your Savior, came for the precise purpose of seeking and saving the lost. He is the light that shines in the darkness, and no darkness can overcome Him. Jesus is with you in your reality. Even the darkness is not dark to Him. Your loving God will never let hurt-filled reality be the sole player on life's stage. His gift of restoration will always show up.

A straying King David saw this truth unfold during an ugly episode of his life. David descended into terrible wrongdoing. He lured a married woman into having an affair with him. The woman, Bathsheba, became pregnant. David, feeling guilty and nervous about his treachery, plotted and orchestrated the murder of Uriah, Bathsheba's husband. Then David took Bathsheba as his wife. David abused his power. He dishonored the trust of the people he led and the God he served.

That's when God stepped in. The opening line of 2 Samuel 12 says, "And the LORD sent Nathan to David." Nathan was a trusted confidant of David and an upright prophet of God. He told the king a story about a rich man whose wealth was abundant and who had no shortage of resources. The rich man lived in the same town as a very poor man. This poor man had only one little ewe lamb to his name. The lamb drank from his cup, shared his food, and slept in his arms. Nathan told King David that the little lamb "was like a daughter" (v. 3) to the poor man. One day, a guest came to visit the rich man. Wanting to be a good host, the rich man decided to prepare a meal for his visitor. But instead of taking one of his own animals, the rich man took the poor man's precious lamb, killed it, and made it the main course of his guest's meal.

King David was outraged when he heard this story. He immediately said to Nathan, "As the LORD lives, the man who has done this deserves to die, and he shall restore the lamb fourfold, because he did this thing, and because he had no pity" (2 Samuel 12:5–6). Nathan looked at David and said, "You are the man!"

Reality hit David with full force. Because of Nathan's words, the king was shattered into pieces. Your heartbreak may not be linked at all to a lack of integrity like David's, but comprehending the enormity of a heartrending issue in your life is something you understand. Perhaps a doctor or a veterinarian brought you face-to-face with a grim reality, or a judge issued a difficult ruling, or an employer spoke words of finality you never thought you would hear. Perhaps an event or the passage of time or even a loved one caused a hurtful reality to shock your heart. In whatever way reality may have hit home in your life, you feel its hurt and sting. And because reality always hits hard, you need a soft place to land. That is why God is relentless about providing restoration in the midst of crushing reality.

Notice that God *sent* Nathan. King David's misdeeds would catch up with him sooner or later. His conscience would begin to crush him. Sin's consequences always boil over when left to simmer. Deep sadness and heartbreak have similar behavior. They don't retreat. They linger, loiter, and lurk with relentless tenacity. There's no way to get away from the difficult reality. That's why God is intentional about sending the gift of restoration.

Nathan brought the truth, but more important, after David realized his need to repent and was brought back to a posture of humility before God, Nathan was present to bring God's lifeline of restoration. The exchange between the truth-telling prophet and the brokenhearted and broken-spirited king went like this: "David said to Nathan, 'I have sinned against the LORD.' And Nathan said to David, 'The LORD also has put away your sin; you shall not die' " (2 Samuel 12:13). It was a glimmer of God's grace when all looked lost. David had to traverse the trying territory of guilt, the loss of his child, and public scorn, but God brought life-restoring help. He does exactly that for the most-broken people.

RESTORATION

When reality hits home, God sends His help. He will walk with you to bear your burden. He will stand with you in the silence of sadness. He will carry you in His arms. We're told about Jesus, the Suffering Servant, in Isaiah 53, "He was despised and rejected by men, a man of sorrows and acquainted with grief" (v. 3). He understands your heartbreak. And even more, He shoulders the burden. Isaiah goes on, "Surely He has borne our griefs and carried our sorrows" (v. 4). The name *Nathan* means "gift." God sent His gift to King David. In your heartbreak, God sends the gift of His only Son. He sends the Good Shepherd, who restores your soul. He sends real strength in Jesus, who conquered the most difficult obstacles imaginable. When Jesus becomes part of any reality, you always have hope.

Words for Healing

Devotion Guide for Chapter Twenty-One

READ Psalm 23

REFLECT

This is one of the most well-known and beloved psalms in the Bible. How do verses 1–3 offer help and hope in your reality?

Verse 4 talks about very difficult times. How have you seen God come through during your challenges?

Verses 5–6 bring reassurance for the present and into eternity. How do these words put your reality into perspective?

PRAY to your Good Shepherd, letting Him know how you need your soul restored. Read through Psalm 23, using each verse to bring God your prayers of thanksgiving and need.

Self

WHEN YOU DON'T KNOW WHO YOU ARE ANYMORE

As [Jesus] drew near to the gate of the town, behold, a
man who had died was being carried out, the only son
of his mother, and she was a widow, and a considerable
crowd from the town was with her. (Luke 7:12)

YOUR STATUS

Life's losses can trigger identity crises. When you're no longer in
a relationship, who do you become? When you're not part of a group
anymore, where do you belong? When a different season of life has
forcefully descended on you, how can you understand or embrace
your new role? When you've been thrown a cruel curve, how is it
possible to still be you?

Your heartbreak may make you feel as if you are disappearing
under its oppressive heaviness. You may feel as if your identity is
fading away behind new labels thrust upon you by your circumstances. Who are you? What should your social media status be? Do you
have the heart to change it? How can you accept the identity grief
has handed to you? Do you even know who you are?

DISAPPEARING

A broken and weeping woman in Luke 7 had a clear understanding of what you are going through: a struggle with grief-stolen identity. Jesus saw the woman accompanied by a crowd of her neighbors
and friends as they left the town of Nain. She and the somber group
walked beside the casket of her only son. The Bible doesn't give the
woman's name. It only adds a grim and disheartening detail about
this mother who lost her one and only son: she was a widow. During
that time and in that place, those two labels of loss were enough to
steal this dear woman's identity. For all practical purposes, her journey of heartbreak caused her to disappear. She was now a childless
widow. That meant she had no heir, no way to support herself, no

social standing, no rights in the eyes of rulers, and no access to spiritual support. Losing her son broke the last straw of her survival. A cascade of new labels began to crash into who she once was. At one time, she was a wife and mother. She enjoyed family and fostered relationships. She possessed resources and pressed into a hopeful future. Now she was alone, poor, unfortunate, destitute, helpless, unwanted, and disconnected. As the crowd carried her son's body past the city gate, the woman wept because of her present sadness and the prospect of her life's total collapse.

It hurts so much to feel like you've lost yourself. When who you were or wanted to be is taken away by unwanted changes, you're left in limbo, wondering if you have any desire—or if there is any possibility—to reinvent your life. You don't know who you are now, and you question if you ever will. But it is precisely at that confusing low point when Jesus saw the disappearing woman from Nain. Luke tells us, "And when the Lord saw her, He had compassion on her and said to her, 'Do not weep'" (Luke 7:13).

SEEN

Jesus *saw* her. When the rest of the world was ready to write her off, Jesus was preparing to give her special attention. When she thought she would never ever see an inkling of hope, Jesus was stepping forward to give her one of His greatest miracles. Please realize that the town of Nain was not on a major thoroughfare. The little village located at the top of a hill was not on the way to anything, and Jesus didn't just happen to pass by. He went there intentionally. Jesus sought out the funeral procession and climbed that hill toward Nain to find the lost and despairing woman. God's true character can be seen clearly when you observe the heart and actions of Jesus. He found her; He saw her; He had compassion on her; and He consoled her.

If you ever wonder how God feels toward you when you're heartbroken, when you're despairing, or when you feel like a mess, please take note. When you're down and out, God does not get disgusted. When you are helpless and immobilized, God does not become impatient with you. In your lowest moments of weakness, God doesn't grit His teeth and tolerate you as a bothersome inconvenience. When you are needy, God doesn't complain about your lack of toughness or grumble that you are taking too much of His time. His heart goes out to you. Compassion wells up within Him. Kindness and concern collect in the depths of His being and spill out in tender and restoring action. God's Word describes His demeanor toward fragile followers like us: "As a father shows compassion to his children, so the LORD shows compassion to those who fear Him" (Psalm 103:13).

Consider what Jesus did for the woman in Nain. After He saw her, approached her, and spoke words of comfort, Jesus touched the casket and stopped the pallbearers in their tracks. Then He did something the woman never could have imagined. Luke 7 describes it well: "[Jesus] said, 'Young man, I say to you, arise.' And the dead man sat up and began to speak, and Jesus gave him to his mother" (vv. 14–15).

God sees you. He approaches you in your adversity. He draws close to restore you. God gets involved. He is not an antagonist intent on making your life difficult. He is the one who renews your identity, calls you by name, and raises you to life. God's foolproof identity-theft protection is the resurrection. In Christ, you are a new creation. You may not see the resurrection of the precious part of life you lost, but you will experience the resurrection of your heart, your life, your hope, your faith, and your being. When you are clothed with Christ in Baptism, there is never a doubt about who you are or whose you are. Only one label prevails in your heartbreak: the God who sacrificed His one and only Son for you has made you His precious and resurrected child.

The crowd in Nain was astounded. We are told that "they glorified God, saying, 'A great prophet has arisen among us!' and 'God has visited His people!'" (Luke 7:16). When you don't know who you are, God visits you and gives you an identity that cannot be taken away. With a touch, a word, and a gift, Jesus brought a mother and son back from the dead. Jesus' touch, His Word, and His ongoing gifts bring you that same new life today.

WORDS FOR HEALING
Devotion Guide for Chapter Twenty-Two

READ Isaiah 43:1–7

REFLECT

Verses 1–2 of this comforting section of Scripture speak powerfully to your identity as you travel through turbulent times. What statements stand out to you as you struggle with a new season of life during loss?

How does God's identity in verse 3 address your deepest needs?

Verses 3–7 express how God feels about us and how He will restore His people from captivity. What expressions of God's comfort, care, and sacrifice provide new insight into your identity?

PRAY a prayer of thanks that God gave His Son in exchange for your life. Use these Scripture verses to talk to God about the new identity He has given you. Ask Him to increase your confidence and clarity about who He has created you to be—even as you experience heartbreak.

Self

WHEN YOU'RE ASHAMED

[The scribes and Pharisees] said to Him, "Teacher,
this woman has been caught in the act of adultery.
Now in the Law, Moses commanded us to stone
such women. So what do You say?" (John 8:4–5)

SHAME

As you reflect on your broken heart, are you becoming convinced
that the life you enjoyed may have been a fluke, something you never
should have had? Do you feel like you never deserved to receive anything good? Perhaps you wonder if your misery and sadness are what
you should have had all along.

Stop! Go no further on this train of misleading thought that
brings you to misplaced misery. Guilt sneaks into your life when you
experience loss, but its secret companion is shame. Guilt says you
did something wrong, but shame declares that you are undeserving
of being loved and unworthy of being blessed. Shame wants you to
believe that nothing good or fulfilling or joyful or right should be
in your life. Why? Because, shame alleges, you're not good enough
for that. Shame is a hazard of heartbreak. It is the self-critical and
self-destructive conviction that you should never have received anything good in the first place. Shame takes your flaws and twists them
into unforgivable sins. Shame takes your mistakes and makes them
out to be mortal disqualifications. Shame loves to leech onto a heart
that is enduring loss. But Jesus has an answer for the sham of shame.

SHAME'S UNDOING

A woman burdened by shame was tossed at Jesus' feet as He
taught in the temple. The episode unfolded in John 8: "The scribes
and the Pharisees brought a woman who had been caught in adultery,
and placing her in the midst they said to Him, 'Teacher, this woman
has been caught in the act of adultery. Now in the Law, Moses com-

manded us to stone such women. So what do You say?' " (vv. 3–5).

The religious leaders were trying to trip Jesus up. They were using a broken and vulnerable woman to advance their own misguided self-righteousness. Yes, the woman was guilty. She was wrong. She violated the sacred gift of marriage and the Law of Moses. But along with the accurate accusation, shame was hurled at her, telling her she didn't deserve to live. The stones to follow would be the exclamation point to the execution of her soul that already transpired.

Jesus quietly bent down and wrote on the ground as the mob continued to badger Him for an answer. After a few moments, Jesus stood up and said, "Let him who is without sin among you be the first to throw a stone at her" (John 8:7). Then He bent down again and continued to write on the ground. Slowly, the crowd began to disperse. We're told that the oldest among the accusers left first. One by one, the bullying group disappeared until Jesus was left alone with the frightened woman.

Some speculate that Jesus may have been writing the names and sins of the woman's accusers in the dust that day. It could be that He was jotting down the Ten Commandments so everyone would remember the whole Law, not just the part they preferred. One thing is clear: the Savior who came to seek and save the lost brought the clarity of God's heart to the cloudy lies of shame. Our abundant misdeeds and mess-ups make a solid case that we deserve nothing good, but the unwavering love of God tells us, "There is therefore now no condemnation for those who are in Christ Jesus" (Romans 8:1). Jesus pulled the plug on shame with unwavering commitment to His purpose.

So Jesus stood up and said, "Woman, where are they? Has no one condemned you?" The woman replied, "No one, Lord." Jesus then spoke words of guiding grace. He diffused shame with God's unconditional love and life-transforming truth. He sent the woman to live a renewed life filled with God's gift of forgiveness. Jesus said, "Neither do I condemn you; go, and from now on sin no more" (John 8:10–11).

SENT

I hope you noticed that Jesus let everyone live. The collection of sinners gathered around Him was neither cursed nor condemned.

Jesus sent each one of them on their way to live new lives. It is true that every person involved in that unruly unrest was guilty of something. They all did wrong. But Jesus didn't let shame prevail. No one deserved kindness, leniency, or grace, but Jesus set a new standard—a shameless standard. He established the irrefutable fact that, in spite of our sin, God loves us. He chooses to love us. We know God's love because Jesus gave His life for us. Shame was banished by God's love. The Scriptures say that we look to "Jesus, the founder and perfecter of our faith, who for the joy that was set before Him endured the cross, despising the shame, and is seated at the right hand of the throne of God" (Hebrews 12:2). Shame met its match at the cross. In Christ, you are worthy to receive good things, God's good things. As the apostle Paul declared, "He who did not spare His own Son but gave Him up for us all, how will He not also with Him graciously give us all things?" (Romans 8:32).

You may be able to think of many reasons you don't deserve anything but heartbreak. But because of God's love and commitment to you, you are worthy of heart-mending and fulfilling joy. You deserve the best because God earned the best for you. Jesus not only sends you away from sin, but from self-critical destruction. You can live your life with hope and go your way with God's goodness because you are considered worthy of new life by God's great grace.

WORDS FOR HEALING
Devotion Guide for Chapter Twenty-Three

READ Psalm 25:1–10

REFLECT

How do verses 1–3 direct you as you wrestle with shame during your time of loss?

Verses 4–5 ask God for teaching and leadership. What unique instruction do you receive from God compared to what the world or your broken heart tell you?

How do verses 6–10 fortify your heart as you face the challenges of guilt and shame on your road of grief?

PRAY words of trust to God. Let Him know why He is trustworthy during your struggles. Thank Him for His enduring mercy and steadfast love and how you've seen those gifts in your life. Lift up your soul to God, and ask Him to restore you.

Self

WHEN YOU SEEM INSIGNIFICANT

Now when Jesus was at Bethany in the house of
Simon the leper, a woman came up to Him with
an alabaster flask of very expensive ointment, and
she poured it on His head as He reclined at table.
And when the disciples saw it, they were indignant,
saying, "Why this waste?" (Matthew 26:6–8)

TOO SMALL?

A man told me with firm resolve and confidence that he didn't
pray because his issues and needs were much too small. He felt it
was inappropriate to pester God with matters of unimportance. A
woman shared that even though she struggled with burdens and
sadness, she kept quiet about her suffering because her problems
seemed insignificant compared to the major concerns raging in the
world. "Who am I," she asked, "to expect anyone to pay attention to
me? I'm just a nobody."

It's tempting to believe that you are small and insignificant, especially in our bigger-than-life celebrity culture. Significance begins
to be measured by the number of followers you have on social media,
name recognition by the public, star status in sports or entertain-
ment, or whether you have world-class wealth. And when heartbreak
hits, your sense of insignificance can grow. You wonder if you deserve any attention at all or if your problems matter to anyone in a
big, busy, and complicated world. Do your loss and sadness have any
significance, you wonder, when everyone else is overloaded by their
own issues? Is your heartbreak worth anyone's attention?

THE GREAT REVERSAL

The overtasked and cluttered world might very well brush you
off. But the One who handles heartbreak does not play by the world's
rules. Jesus gives us a glimpse into God's standard of significance.

The Savior said, "For he who is least among you all is the one who is great" (Luke 9:48). Jesus said that the first shall be last and the last shall be first. He lauded the growth power of tiny mustard seeds and lifted up the immense value of little children. One glance through God's lens puts everything in proper perspective. Your struggles matter. Your sadness is significant. Your heartbreak is a deep concern of God's heart. When you feel like you don't matter, God chimes in and says, "Yes, you do."

An example of this great reversal unfolded during a fascinating episode in Jesus' life. He and His disciples were at the house of a man called Simon the leper. To be in the home of someone who was shunned because of this dreaded illness is itself a dramatic reversal. But while Jesus and His followers were there, a woman approached Jesus with a jar of expensive ointment. As Jesus reclined at Simon's table, the woman poured the aromatic oil over Jesus' head. The disciples couldn't believe what they were seeing. Outraged, they said, "Why this waste? For this could have been sold for a large sum and given to the poor" (Matthew 26:8–9). Their outburst belittled the woman, called into question her intent, and marginalized her loving generosity. The assertion of the disciples relegated the woman to insignificance.

Imagine how she felt at that moment. You may understand very well. When you've shared your struggle with a friend, you may have been counseled to "get over it." After pouring out your anguish to someone close to you, the listener may have replied by brushing your suffering aside to recite a litany of her own problems and issues. After your experience of loss, a person in your life may have told you that "it could be worse." It doesn't feel good to be belittled. But people don't always handle hearts very well.

As the woman's heart lay exposed to public criticism, Jesus spoke up. He said to the disgusted disciples, "Why do you trouble the woman? For she has done a beautiful thing to Me. For you always have the poor with you, but you will not always have Me. In pouring this ointment on My body, she has done it to prepare Me for burial. Truly, I say to you, wherever this gospel is proclaimed in the whole world, what she has done will also be told in memory of her" (Matthew 26:10–13).

Jesus took a woman consigned to irrelevance and connected

her deed to the heart of God's plan. He elevated a woman who was cast aside to the position of being someone whose action would be remembered until His return. It was Christ's classic great reversal: "Everyone who exalts himself will be humbled, and he who humbles himself will be exalted" (Luke 14:11). What was seen as insignificant was, in reality, of the greatest importance.

The same is true for you. Your heartbreak is God's greatest and most pressing issue. Your brokenness is God's utmost concern. God so loved the world, that He gave His one and only Son. If the world's population consisted of only you, God wouldn't have changed a thing. He would have given His all to rescue, redeem, and restore you. That is how significant you are. Your significance isn't equal to the number of people who like you; it is equal to the immensity of God's love for you. In Jesus, your significance is certain.

CALL WITH CONFIDENCE

So God says, "Call upon Me in the day of trouble; I will deliver you, and you shall glorify Me" (Psalm 50:15). Because of God's love for you and Jesus' intimate understanding of your struggles, God's Word invites us: "Let us then with confidence draw near to the throne of grace, that we may receive mercy and find grace to help in time of need" (Hebrews 4:16).

For every need, with every trouble, in all heartbreak, and as you suffer loss, you are invited to pour out your soul to your Savior, who considers your life and your cares to be of the greatest significance. There is no detail too small and no sadness too trivial that would prevent you from approaching God with courage and confidence. Your life is at the heart of God's plan. You are important to Jesus. After all, He shed His blood for you. You are esteemed by the One who matters most. You've got God's undivided attention.

WORDS FOR HEALING
Devotion Guide for Chapter Twenty-Four

READ Psalm 9:1–10

REFLECT

These verses recount the deeds of the Lord in the face of struggle. How do you relate to the struggles mentioned?

How have you seen God respond to your deepest needs and cares?

How do verses 9–10 sum up God's attitude toward you?

PRAY to the Stronghold for the oppressed, letting Him know what troubles you at this time in your life. Ask Him not to forsake you in specific areas of worry and stress. Thank Him for valuing your life and blessing you with eternal hope.

Self

WHEN YOU'RE TIRED OF CRYING

[The woman said of Jesus,] "If I touch even His garments, I will be made well." (Mark 5:28)

NO MORE TEARS

Are you tired of tears? Do you feel like placing your flood of sadness on pause? Are you ready for some rest? Are your puffy eyes, stuffy nose, overloaded emotions, and overwhelmed mind telling you that you need a break from what breaks your heart? How can you find a window of rest from hurt that not only stays with you but seems to grow as time goes by?

A woman in Mark 5 was in that place. Weary of weeping, she finally said, "Enough." She fought through a throng of people around Jesus to touch His robe. After suffering for twelve years with an illness that caused her to bleed, after spending all her money on doctor after doctor who offered no solution, and after seeing her malady become worse instead of better, the woman became fed up with fighting. Instead of being lost in her tears, she wanted to be found and at peace. So she sought help from the One who was working miracles. Approaching Jesus, she said, "If I touch even His garments, I will be made well." Making her way through the crowd, the woman came up behind Jesus, stretched out her hand, and touched His clothes. Mark tells us that "immediately the flow of blood dried up, and she felt in her body that she was healed of her disease" (Mark 5:29). After twelve long years of stress and strain, freedom had come. Finally, joy and relief replaced sadness and pain. There were no more tears.

In a miraculous and unexplainable way, Jesus provides that rest and freedom. This may be one of the greatest gifts from the One who carried your sorrows and shouldered your pain in His own suffering on the cross. Having overcome the power of sadness and loss in His resurrection, Jesus is able to press pause during times of pain so you can be replenished by seasons of peace. He carries your heartbreak so you can rest. He stops your tears—even for a few moments—to provide some restoring moments of joy.

A CLAMORING CROWD

A crowd of obstacles will try to stand in the way of Jesus' healing. A throng of thoughts and feelings will attempt to keep you from a life of freedom. You may feel like you're strong enough to handle your own pain, so you hunker down and try to tough it out. You might get busy and stuff your sadness inside. Experts talk about the stages of grief, so you may try to work through those to "get it over with." You may lean into self-help advice or other ancient methods of achieving peace. But like the woman who struggled with her troubled life in the Gospel of Mark, personal efforts won't bring lasting peace, and the solutions generated by the world will cause heartbreak to grow worse.

That's why it is so good to hear about Jesus. The woman heard about Him. Jesus was doing what no one else could accomplish. He healed people. He encouraged the broken and gave hope to the hopeless. He paid attention to the outcast and brought mercy to the wounded. The woman probably wondered, "Why couldn't it be me?" So she squirmed through the crowd that blocked her way in order to access just a small sampling of Jesus' help and blessing. One touch, and she was healed. A simple touch did in seconds what twelve years of torturous trying couldn't do.

PEACE

God's Word calls this "the peace of God, which surpasses all understanding" (Philippians 4:7). It isn't peace generated by us. It is peace that is unexplainable. When the turbulence of grief and struggle swirl and rage in your heart and soul, Jesus calms the storm. Everything may still be unsettled. Solutions and resolution may still elude you. But somehow, in some mysterious way, Jesus gives you a break from your tears and fills you with peace. It's not self-help; it's God's help. This is what the woman in Mark 5 experienced in a powerful way. It's what Jesus speaks into your life too. He said, "Peace I leave with you; My peace I give to you. Not as the world gives do I give to you. Let not your hearts be troubled, neither let them be afraid" (John 14:27).

Jesus means what He says. He gives freedom from gloom through His living Word and lasting presence. He takes your heavy burden and gives you a light load to carry. He rescues you from raging flood-waters and leads you to lie down by quiet streams so your weary soul can be restored. He leads you through the wilderness to life-nourishing green pastures. No one else can provide such peace.

After the woman was healed, Jesus knew "that power had gone out from Him" (Mark 5:30). He turned around in the crowd and searched for the person who touched His garment. His disciples told Him that too many people were pressing around Him to sense the touch of one person. How could He ask, "Who touched Me?" (v. 31). But Jesus searched. That's what He does for the heartbroken who need healing. He searches for you. He sees you. Seeing His gaze, the woman came to Jesus with fear and trembling. She told Him every-thing—the whole story of her powerlessness, her struggle, the dis-appointment with doctors, and the futility of the last twelve years. Jesus replied, "Daughter, your faith has made you well; go in peace, and be healed of your disease" (v. 34).

A displaced woman who was considered unclean because of her bleeding was now called "daughter." A person who was weary from tears and hopelessness became someone who possessed the gift of life-transforming faith. Peace came along with her healing. Weari-ness and weeping were put on hold so she could again experience a life of wholeness.

You can too. The grief that grows heavy in your hands finds life and hope when Jesus holds it. In a miraculous and heart-reviving way, God's got this. He provides a needed break when you're tired of crying.

WORDS FOR HEALING
Devotion Guide for Chapter Twenty-Five

READ Psalm 116

REFLECT

The first four verses of this psalm contrast the gift of God's peace with the anguish brought on by our broken world. What has the world been doing to compound your grief, and how is God helping you?

How do verses 5–9 give you insight into how you receive rest now and how you receive hope that lasts forever?

Verses 10–19 speak of gratitude in the middle of affliction. What reasons do you have to give thanks to God even as you struggle?

PRAY a prayer of thanksgiving, letting God know why you are thankful as He walks with you in your grief.

Self

WHEN YOU CAN'T GET OUT OF BED

[Elijah] asked that he might die, saying, "It is
enough; now, O LORD, take away my life, for I am
no better than my fathers." (1 Kings 19:4)

THE DARK NIGHT OF THE SOUL

People trapped in depressing sadness have described their experience as feeling numb, empty, and paralyzed. They have portrayed
their struggle as a heavy gray haze that closes in on them and doesn't
relent. Nothing seems bright or real. No energy or excitement can be
found. At best, they are going through the motions. At worst, they
are falling into a deep pit, feeling as if there is no help and no hope
for any kind of future. This is the dark night of the soul that saps your
strength and robs you of any desire—and ability—to get out of bed
in the morning.

Heartbreak can trigger depression. Chemicals that are normally flowing in balanced harmony become jumbled by stress, upheaval,
and sadness. Your whole system is shocked and traumatized. You feel
the physical impact of a stunned mind and wounded heart. Grief af-
fects the whole person. Counseling and medication may be essential
elements of your road to healing. If your depression is clinical, there
is no way you can pull your way out of it, think your way out of it, or
power your way out of it. Even if your lingering lethargy and sadness
do not fall into the category of a clinical diagnosis, you still need help
beyond yourself. You need a hand up from someone who isn't beaten
down by heartbreak.

PROVISION FOR YOUR JOURNEY

Take Elijah's word for it. He tried to work his way out of grief but
ended up even deeper in despair. After evil Queen Jezebel threatened his life, Elijah ran away into the desert. He isolated himself, exhausted himself, and criticized himself. He was convinced he was a

failure. Elijah cried out to God, "It is enough; now, O LORD, take away my life, for I am no better than my fathers." Then he collapsed and fell asleep. He didn't have the energy to get up or to get going.

You may feel the same way. You have absolutely no desire or energy to tackle any tasks, meet any friends, say any prayers, or think about any possibility of a future. It's not that you're a quitter or weak or lacking ambition. No, it's not about any deficiency on your part. It is about being deeply wounded and stricken by loss.

Is there an answer? Fighting exhaustion will only exhaust you further. But feeding exhaustion and sadness with God's food of rest and replenishment will drain grief's power and erase its energy. Consider Elijah's journey. As he lay paralyzed in the wilderness of woundedness, God fed him with warm baked bread and rehydrated him with a jug of fresh water. Then Elijah went back to bed. A second time, God gently nudged him and gave him a replenishing meal. Only after repeated rest and nourishment did Elijah have the strength to continue his journey through the wilderness. Please take note: God's provision didn't take Elijah out of his wilderness; it sustained him along the way. There may very well be a day when you spring out of bed feeling like the "old" you. But another scenario looms before you: you may never feel "normal" or "good" again. Your journey may be a wilderness journey from this point forward. But while every voice in the world might tell you either to hurry up and get better or to keep your distance and not bring them down, God touches you with urgent gentleness and implores you not to give up hope. He will nourish you along the way. He will provide sustenance in your wilderness of sadness and loss.

God said to His weary and ragged people in Isaiah 30, "In returning and rest you shall be saved; in quietness and in trust shall be your strength" (v. 15). It may feel like people and life itself are pushing you away, but God will always draw you close. It's no accident that Jesus called Himself the bread of life and living water. When Jesus reinforced the fact that people cannot live on bread alone but receive restored life from the Word that proceeds from the mouth of God, He was outlining the essential menu for exhausted travelers. Just as you return to the dining-room table or your favorite restaurant for steady sustenance, God brings you back to His gustatory grace so the wilderness of this world won't overcome you. Moment by moment, breath by breath, hour by hour, day by day, your Savior will sustain you. Even when you can't find the strength to speak, He hears the groans from the depths of your heart and soul. In your stunned silence and sadness, God speaks up to bring you consolation from His Word. Just think, Jesus knew you would need to be nourished along the way. He gave His sustaining meal of life when He said, "Take and eat; take and drink." God isn't a fair-weather friend; He is trudging through the trenches of heartbreak with you.

EMBRACED BY GRACE

If you feel like you can't get out of bed, take a deep breath and let God know. Admit your heartbreak. Confess your sadness. Pour out your heart to God. Lie in the darkness and ask Him for help. Embrace your dark night of the soul. Let Jesus know that He'd better do something because you can't do anything. Lean hard into God's arms; when you do, you will be embraced by His grace.

Take life one heartbeat at a time. Let each step be enough. Lean on a trusted friend or a compassionate counselor who can share the burdens of your heart and soul. Ask God to open doors of help and restoration. Patiently watch and wait.

Then, don't fret about the future. Resist thinking about tomorrow. Fight the urge to fast-forward to what your life may be like in the long haul. Press pause on worrying about how or if your feelings of woe will be fixed. There's a better way. When you can't get out of bed, fall into the care of the One who knows how to bring you through the worst wilderness. You may not get over it, but God will get you through it.

WORDS FOR HEALING

Devotion Guide for Chapter Twenty-Six

READ Psalm 40:1–3

REFLECT

What does verse 1 tell you about the timing and duration of your struggle and God's presence and activity along the way?

What mud, mire, and bog are bogging you down (as v. 2 mentions), and how have you seen God give you firm ground on which to stand as you journey through heartbreak?

The new song mentioned in verse 3 means that an old tune of worry, hopelessness, and sadness has been replaced by new lyrics. What new reasons for hope can you "sing" about because of God's nourishing grace in your life?

PRAY a prayer that tells God your old song and recounts the new song He's given you. Ask Him to keep you singing even as the dark clouds of loss still surround you.

Self

WHEN YOUR STRUGGLE DOESN'T GO AWAY

After this many of [Jesus'] disciples turned back and
no longer walked with Him. So Jesus said to the twelve,
"Do you want to go away as well?" (John 6:66–67)

NEVER

A friend of mine could not have children, even though she and
her husband wanted to so desperately. They tried every medical solution possible. They made sincere attempts at adoption, but time kept
passing and the possibility of parenting ebbed away. As advancing
years went on, the fact that they would never be a mom and dad
became set in the unforgiving cement of the march of time. Never
would the yearning of their hearts be met. Never would their struggle diminish.

The same was true of a friend who endured chronic pain. That
word—*chronic*—can be a life sentence to ongoing misery. It's true
of too many situations. The trials of depression, forced retirement,
a prodigal and resistant son or daughter, and the breakup of your
family may never see complete resolution. Your sadness and grief in
those and other heartbreaking struggles may never go away.

The word *never* is frightening. It is not an emotional place you
would ever want to go. Never? Chronic? Lasting? Enduring? Persistent? No answer? It's here to live with for good? In a world that is
intent on finding the cure for everything, facing question marks and
shrugged shoulders from experts can crush your spirit and lead you
to despair. When you won't get "better" and your situation is not expected to improve, what do you do? When you get to the point of realizing that your struggle will always be present in this "vale of tears,"
where do you turn? Do you have any recourse or any source of hope?

A CAPABLE COMPANION

A number of years ago, my wife and I, along with our two daughters, traveled to West Africa to visit and work alongside friends who

lived there. After a couple of weeks teaching and serving with our friends in the wild wilderness of Africa, we bade them farewell and began our trip home. That's when the journey became harrowing. Our plane's takeoff was aborted as an engine failed and the threat of a fire developed. We were evacuated from the aircraft. Then, as we trudged back to the terminal, we heard that the airline workers decided to go on strike. Employees stopped work immediately; tensions were high. We sat on the open tarmac and sought refuge from the sun in an open-air seating area as soldiers armed with automatic weapons milled about. We had no food, no water, no ability to communicate with anyone in the outside world, and no opportunity to sleep. Hours passed until we were finally herded into buses and taken to an old hotel in the middle of a bustling urban area. We were warned to stay off the streets and beware of strangers. No updates from the airline were provided. The only indication of the reality of our situation was the sign in the lobby of the hotel: "Timbuktu." Yes, we were where my mother warned she would send us if we didn't behave. We were in the middle of absolute uncertainty.

But a glimmer of light shone in that unsure darkness. Her name was Nancy. She was a missionary nurse who knew the local languages and customs. She had been in this country before. She knew the airport and the city. She translated for us, guided us along the unfamiliar way, and even helped us laugh. It took us eighty-four hours to get from West Africa to Paris, but we didn't have to endure the long and seemingly interminable struggle alone.

The truth you need when your struggle doesn't go away is this: While a brutal journey can break you, a capable companion will buoy you along the way. Your companion's name is Jesus. He is the light who shines in your darkness—even when the gloomy clouds of struggle will not break this side of heaven. Jesus has been where you are. He knows the foreign land in which you find yourself. He understands the abrasiveness of your ongoing heartbreak. He traveled the road of sorrows that led to more sorrows. His life's pursuit pointed toward death—and He knew it all along. If you know Jesus' story, you know the rejection, the threats, the cruelty and criticism, the scorn and skepticism, the temptation and the torture He endured. Jesus understands struggle that takes its time, taunts you, and tempers your sense of joy. He can appreciate your helplessness as you face unrelenting pain. He is a capable companion. Referring to Jesus, the Book of Hebrews says, "For we do not have a high priest who is unable to sympathize with our weaknesses, but one who in every respect has been tempted as we are, yet without sin" (4:15).

Jesus has been in your shoes. He has walked through your wilderness. He is your capable companion because He knows the way and has what it takes to bring you through your grief. Along the way, He can interpret the strange dialect of struggle. He can point out how even the wilderness keeps you close to Him. He leads you in a sour but sweet companionship that fills you up in a mysterious and challenging yet beautiful way. And He promises to sustain you and bring you through. Jesus' resurrection from death is the guarantee. When Jesus is your companion, He won't let your ship languish in the open seas of uncertainty; He will bring you to the safe haven of restored life that lasts forever.

TO WHOM SHALL WE GO?

At one point during Jesus' ministry, many people who followed Him, cheered Him on, and endorsed Him walked away. With what sounds like grief and heartbreak, Jesus turned to His twelve disciples and asked, "Do you want to go away as well?" (John 6:67). It was a decisive moment. The Twelve were confused, uncertain, and mystified about Jesus' teaching in that instant. They weren't clear about what the future held. But Peter spoke up and said, "Lord, to whom shall we go? You have the words of eternal life, and we have believed, and have come to know, that You are the Holy One of God" (John 6:68–69). Who else could give them hope? Where else could they find help?

That is the verdict of the hymn that contains the phrase "vale of tears." Jesus is the companion who will bring you through struggles that won't go away. This stanza of the hymn "Be Still, My Soul" says:

> Be still, my soul; though dearest friends depart And all is darkened in this vale of tears;
>
> Then you will better know His love, His heart, Who comes to soothe your sorrows and your fears.
>
> Be still, my soul; your Jesus can repay From His own fullness all He takes away. (*LSB* 752:3)

WORDS FOR HEALING
Devotion Guide for Chapter Twenty-Seven

READ Psalm 138

REFLECT

How does the author's reflection on God's action in verses 1–3 help strengthen your faith in God's responsiveness to your needs?

If all the kings of the earth will sing of God's ways (vv. 4–5), what does that tell you about God's dependability in your struggles?

Verses 6–8 bring a strong message of comfort for ongoing struggles. How do these verses encourage you and give you confidence?

PRAY through verses 7–8, sharing your specific troubles with God, thanking Him for the ways you've seen His presence and steadfast love, and asking Him to fulfill His purpose for you.

Self
WHEN YOU HATE YOUR SITUATION

And the LORD said to me, "Go again, love a woman
who is loved by another man and is an adulteress,
even as the LORD loves the children of Israel,
though they turn to other gods." (Hosea 3:1)

HATING LIFE

Sometimes, you hate your life. You hate the heartbreak that col-
lided with you head-on. You despise your situation. You don't like
the season you're in, and you wonder if you will ever be free from the
unrelenting inner ache you feel. Why do you have to go through this?
If you had a choice, you would chuck this circumstance into oblivion.
You hate what's happening and want to leave it behind.

If you stay in this territory of hatred, you may find yourself developing a heart of stone. Symptoms include anger, bitterness, and
cynicism. Kindness will not come easily. Optimism will depart from
your vocabulary and outlook. Take warning: this is no place to stay.

But even if you want to break out of the heartbreak that keeps
closing in on you, there may seem to be no escape. Truth be told, your
wounded reality is, at times, too strong for the relief you crave. Instead, you may find yourself watching the clock tick and seeing each
second escort you into deeper sadness and frustration. Is there any
way to be freed from a situation you despise?

A HEART OF FLESH

Hosea understood what it is like to be trapped in a terrible situation. In his role as a prophet of God, he was commanded to marry a
woman who would be completely unfaithful to him. God said graph-
ically in Hosea 1, "Go, take to yourself a wife of whoredom and have
children of whoredom, for the land commits great whoredom by forsaking the LORD" (v. 2). God's point was to show in a clear and excruciating way that He didn't like *His* situation. God's heart was grieved

after the people He saved, nourished, protected, and nurtured left Him out in the cold by worshiping other gods and living lives absent of His love. God was hurt and heartbroken. He felt betrayed and rejected. His beloved people were cheating on Him. Their self-centered spirits led God to suffer unbearable loss.

So He commissioned Hosea to live the nightmare and show all the people exactly how He felt. You may understand what it feels like to live in a plodding and insufferable nightmare. But while the gravitational pull of your own brokenness may send you plummeting into despair and grumbling, God embarks on a remarkable and unanticipated detour when He agonizes over hated situations. It's a detour that can reroute your heart when you hate your life. You see, God doesn't harden His heart against us when we abandon Him; He opens His heart to hold out hope. When you despise your situation, God is persistent about putting a heart of flesh in you. God's tender words in Ezekiel 36:26 tell us, "I will give you a new heart, and a new spirit I will put within you. And I will remove the heart of stone from your flesh and give you a heart of flesh."

When you hate your situation, God keeps working to give life to your hurting or hardening heart. Have you heard Him calling you back to Himself? Have you witnessed the glimmers of love and hope He places in your life? Sometimes, you feel like you're hanging on by only a thread, but it is a strong and resilient thread of God's persistent grace. Watch. Listen. Be attentive to the seemingly insignificant encounters and the unanticipated conversations. Dive into God's Word, and slowly soak in the love and purpose He has for you. You'll discover some treasures buried in your hated life.

SURPRISING THE WORLD

That's how life unfolded for Hosea. How would his story turn out? Would misery and heartbreak win? No, God wasn't going to let that happen. Instead, He would overwhelm the hated situation with life-transforming love. God spoke surprisingly about His unfaithful people: "Therefore, behold, I will allure her, and bring her into the wilderness, and speak tenderly to her" (Hosea 2:14). Instead of displaying anger, cynicism, and bitterness, God gushed words of passionate affection: "I will betroth you to Me forever. I will betroth you to Me in righteousness and in justice, in steadfast love and in mercy. I will betroth you to Me in faithfulness. And you shall know the LORD" (vv. 19–20). So God told Hosea to woo back his unfaithful wife in order to wow God's unfaithful people with a display of undeserved love. It was a new, unexpected, and surprising beginning.

When you approach your hated situation, determined to demonstrate God's caring approach to you, the world will be stunned by the surprise of God's countercultural quality of grace-filled perseverance. The apostle Paul encouraged his listeners in Galatia, "Let us not grow weary of doing good, for in due season we will reap, if we do not give up" (Galatians 6:9).

Only the Savior can turn a hated situation inside out. Only the Holy Spirit, whose specialty is encouragement, can accomplish the reversal of a sour reality into a sweet opportunity. Only God can give you a heart of flesh that will surprise a world where hearts of stone are mass produced. You've seen it happen. Amish farmers forgive the murderers of their children. A victim of a tragic accident becomes an inspiration in her life as a quadriplegic. An oppressed laborer transforms a coarse context by being a beacon of kindness. An imprisoned felon serves as Jesus' messenger behind bars. A heartbroken woman reaches out in her grief to be a source of help and hope for battered and broken young people. By faith, the greatest grace can flow from the deepest wells of despair.

Your hated situation may be where Jesus needs you most—not because He is playing games with your heart, but so He can shape you and use you to understand and help others in great need. And you are not alone as you struggle through the situation you despise. Jesus is right alongside you. Remember, He asked His Father to remove the situation He faced. He begged that His suffering be stopped. But God needed Him there to save us. Jesus is the source of your vocation in every situation. You are where you are today so you can display the miraculous and beautiful presence of God. How? How can you keep going when you hate your situation? Keep walking with your Savior, who will enliven your heart, open your eyes, and use you to hold out His hope to people in desperate need.

WORDS FOR HEALING
Devotion Guide for Chapter Twenty-Eight

READ Jonah 2

REFLECT

In verses 1–2, we hear that Jonah was in a situation he despised, so he called out to God in prayer. When might you overlook calling on God in your situation, and how could prayer, as a first step, be helpful?

Jonah described the misery of his circumstances in verses 3–6, but he also articulated the glimmer of hope God provided. How can you relate to the details of Jonah's agony, and how are you seeing God's hope these days?

What surprises you, inspires you, and provides guidance for your struggle in verses 7–10?

PRAY like Jonah as you navigate your grief. Talk to God, tell Him how you really feel, recall His love and promises to you, and let Him know that you will follow Him.

Faith
WHEN YOU'RE QUESTIONING GOD

[Habakkuk asked,] "O LORD, how long shall I cry for help,
and You will not hear? Or cry to You 'Violence!' and You
will not save? Why do You make me see iniquity, and
why do You idly look at wrong?" (Habakkuk 1:2–3)

BIG QUESTIONS

What are the questions you have for God? As you contemplate
and confront your sadness, what issues are coursing through your
mind and heart? Do you wonder why your heartbreak happened? Are
you confused about what in the world God was thinking? Are you
trying to figure out where God was in the middle of what caused your
grief? Is He really God at all if He allows such sadness to unfold and
such loss to be permitted? What happened to His alleged love and
care? Why did He let you become broken, and why does He allow
others to be hurt?

Mother Teresa commented that the first thing she would say to
Jesus in heaven would be this: "You've got a lot of explaining to do."
After encountering the ravages of suffering, pain, and injustice, the
compassionate servant who ministered to the broken in Calcutta
could relate to everyone who wonders how a caring God could really
exist in a world where, at times, it seems He is absent and doesn't
care.

The Bible even asks those big questions. Faced with unbearable
injustice and pain, the prophet Habakkuk confronted God by boldly
saying, "O LORD, how long shall I cry for help, and You will not hear?
Or cry to You 'Violence!' and You will not save? Why do You make me
see iniquity, and why do You idly look at wrong? . . . Are You not from
everlasting, O LORD my God, my Holy One? . . . Why do You idly look
at traitors and remain silent when the wicked swallows up the man
more righteous than he?" (Habakkuk 1:2–3, 12–13).

You can easily add your questions to Habakkuk's list. When you experience heartbreak, it is normal to bring your big questions to God: "Do You care about me? Why did You allow this? I thought You were a loving God. Are You or aren't You in control? Why didn't You intervene and do the right thing?"

Will this type of inquiry get you in trouble with God? Will your interrogation lead you to a dangerous place in your faith? Is it okay to challenge God with your big questions?

BRING IT ALL

You might feel uncomfortable confronting God with issues that plague your heart and seem to put His position as the Lord of the universe in jeopardy. It may feel like taboo territory as you take the toughest topics of heartbreak to the Savior who claims to care. You may believe that asking God questions will hurt your relationship with Him or cause Him to cast you aside. But as you struggle to make sense of your senseless heartbreak, God invites you to bring it all to Him: "Call upon Me in the day of trouble; I will deliver you, and you shall glorify Me" (Psalm 50:15). In another psalm, we are told, "Cast your burden on the LORD, and He will sustain you; He will never permit the righteous to be moved" (55:22).

God gives you full permission to pour out your heart to Him and to pose every question you can muster. God wants you to wrestle with Him. He wants you to cry out. He can handle you when you hide nothing from Him. And He hears you. God gives you reassurance about His love and care even when it seems as if He has abandoned you and let the floodgates of unfair loss overwhelm you. The challenge is not necessarily in your questions or in your unleashed emotions toward Him. The big issue is not your inquiry. It is whether you will listen to Him and trust His response. You see, questions posed to God are wasted if you are not attuned to His answers.

GOD'S ANSWERS

After challenging God with his big questions, Habakkuk said, "I will take my stand at my watchpost and station myself on the tower, and look out to see what He will say to me" (Habakkuk 2:1). Habakkuk made a commitment to listen and to watch. How did God answer the frustrated prophet? Not with a detailed outline of how everything would be worked out in the long run. Not with a glimpse into the eternal planning methods of the Almighty. Not even with the reassurance that everything in Habakkuk's life or with Habakkuk's people would turn out all right. God answered with the assurance that His character could be trusted, that His faithfulness would prevail, that He had an amazing plan, and that He would never abandon them.

This brings an important principle to our questioning confrontations: God doesn't always explain, but He does always sustain.

There are some things you will never know or understand. You will never be able to comprehend some mysteries of life's intricate tapestry. Frustration and confusion may linger in your life when you are wounded and life runs counter to your plans, hopes, and dreams. Sometimes, you just won't be able to figure it out. At those times, God asks if you will trust Him. In the middle of your venting, shouting, and questioning, will you trust God even when everything doesn't make sense?

God embraced Habakkuk in his questioning but led him to wait in faith. The prophet closed out his book of the Bible by saying, "Though the fig tree should not blossom, nor fruit be on the vines, the produce of the olive fail and the fields yield no food, the flock be cut off from the fold and there be no herd in the stalls, yet I will rejoice in the LORD; I will take joy in the God of my salvation. GOD, the Lord, is my strength" (Habakkuk 3:17–19). God welcomes your questions and outcries. Even when you don't receive immediate or complete answers, you will receive His immediate and complete care. God sent His Son, Jesus, to hang on the cross and rise from the dead so you would never be left hanging in abandoned uncertainty. Bring everything to God—even your most brutal questions. He will wrap His Word of life around you and will draw close to you, always listening, never letting you go, showing you your next step and your reason for hope.

WORDS FOR HEALING
Devotion Guide for Chapter Twenty-Nine

READ Psalm 6

REFLECT

Several times throughout the Psalms, we hear the question "How long?" How do verses 1–3 reflect the big questions you are asking God?

Verses 4–7 plead with God for His care during excruciating grief. How do these verses capture your feelings, and how could God's care be of help to you in your confusion and pain?

What confidence and hope do verses 8–10 give you in your struggle?

PRAY your big questions to God. Ask Him about everything that causes you doubt and confusion. Cast your cares on Him. Then, let God know you will listen for His answers and watch for His sustaining care.

Faith

WHEN YOU BELIEVE GOD HAS FORGOTTEN YOU

[David said,] "I had said in my alarm, 'I am cut off from
Your sight.' But You heard the voice of my pleas for
mercy when I cried to You for help." (Psalm 31:22)

FORGOTTEN

There are times when it seems as though God has forgotten you.
You pray, but nothing changes. You're being hurt, but the hurting
continues. You're ready for the next step, but all you have to step
into is a void. People around you are making progress, enjoying blessings, and living the life you yearn for. But for some mystifying reason,
you languish in the frustrating sameness of a wearying status quo. It
feels as if the world keeps moving ahead, but you've been overlooked.
Somehow, your page out of God's divine plan seems to have been
shaken loose and has drifted unnoticed to the floor of heaven. Now
you wait and wonder, feeling as if you've been cut off from God's
sight, ignored, unseen, disregarded, and stuck in your loss.

Can God forget about you? Would He? Is He too busy to pay attention to everyone in need? Can you drop from His to-do list and be
left fending for yourself? Can you mess up so badly that God decides
to ignore you?

Those are problems that can plague you when loss barges into
your life. King David asked similar questions when he felt forgotten and completely abandoned by God. David was fifteen years old
when he was anointed to be king of Israel. But after that seminal
moment in his life, David was left to wait. It took fifteen years for
David to be acknowledged as king. During those years, David lived a
life of misery and tumult. He was on the run from threats of death.
He wandered in the wilderness and hid in caves. He eluded capture
by pretending to be insane, throwing aside all dignity to let drool
run down his beard and to laugh like a madman. He fought in wars,

lost his best friend, lived in chaos, faced opposition, felt the fear of danger, and wondered if God had forgotten him.

Can David, in his seasons of feeling forgotten, help unlock the mystery of God's seeming forgetfulness?

WHERE GOD IS

God said about David, "I have found in David the son of Jesse a man after My heart, who will do all My will" (Acts 13:22). David wasn't perfect—far from it. David didn't always listen to God. At times, he became impatient and acted impulsively. Sometimes he wasn't very wise. But David wasn't in the position of waiting for God because he did anything wrong. David didn't linger because God lost control of history. David didn't languish because God didn't have a plan. Even when it seemed to David that he had been forgotten, God was still working faithfully behind the scenes.

The beleaguered king did have times of panic and doubt. He cried out to God in Psalm 31, "I had said in my alarm, 'I am cut off from Your sight.'" David feared God had forgotten him. But then, remembering God's character and promises, he added, "But You heard the voice of my pleas for mercy when I cried to You for help." In fact, David became so encouraged about God's closeness and attentiveness, he could speak the words Jesus used on the cross: "Into Your hand I commit my spirit; You have redeemed me, O LORD, faithful God" (Psalm 31:5). God did not forget about David, no matter how bad things looked. God did not forsake him, no matter how much he hurt. That is why David could close Psalm 31 by saying, "Be strong, and let your heart take courage, all you who wait for the LORD!" (v. 24). It is why he could voice confidently in Psalm 9, "The needy shall not always be forgotten, and the hope of the poor shall not perish forever" (v. 18).

God makes something very clear to you about your situation. He never forgets you. God does not play games with your heart or willingly bring grief into your life. David knew this throughout his odyssey of struggle. When God seemed absent, David knew where God was: always with him as Savior and Comforter. With unwavering confidence, he even called God his shepherd (Psalm 23).

How does this help you? When you're afflicted with grief, you can be certain that you are not forgotten by God. No, you are part of

His bigger plan that ends well. When you feel like you've been over-looked, you can take heart that you haven't dropped off God's radar; you are in the center of His will, cherished and loved each moment by God, who is at your side. He graciously provides help and encour-agement along the way.

This is an important paradigm shift. In your pain, you are not called to concentrate on where God seems absent. Rather, you are directed to take refuge where God is present.

God doesn't give you the cold shoulder because of your imper-fection. He doesn't make you stew while He tries to keep the world's plates spinning. He isn't trying to make things up as He goes along. He isn't struggling to cope with all the surprises you throw at Him. He doesn't lose track of you in a crowded world of people in need. No. God always remembers you. Always. And He is always present, always close. If you can't locate Him in your loss, His comforting presence can be found in His Word. If you can't see Him as you suffer sadness, His promised presence prevails in you through your Baptism. If you feel He is too far away when your heart is broken, He steps into your life over and over again in His Holy Meal, inviting you to "take and eat, take and drink" His body and His blood for your strength and forgiveness.

These are dependable points of refuge where God has located Himself for you. God never forgets you. The only part of your life God doesn't remember is your sins. That's because Jesus was forsak-en on the cross in your place. When your excruciating loss causes you to believe God has forgotten you, see your forgiving, self-sacrificing, dependable, and understanding Savior close by. You can confidently commit yourself into His caring hands.

WORDS FOR HEALING
Devotion Guide for Chapter Thirty

READ Psalm 31:1–5

REFLECT

How does the plea in verses 1–2 show you that God is close to you?

God is described as a rock, fortress, and refuge in verses 3–4. How do these descriptions help you understand God's attitude toward you?

In what ways has God been leading and guiding you through your loss?

PRAY verse 5 of this psalm. Let God know how you see that He has not forgotten you—starting with Jesus' death and resurrection for you. Share your worries and concerns with Him. Let Him know that you commit yourself into His caring hands.

Faith
WHEN YOU'RE ANGRY AT GOD

A Canaanite woman from that region came out and was
crying, "Have mercy on me, O Lord, Son of David; my
daughter is severely oppressed by a demon." But [Jesus]
did not answer her a word. (Matthew 15:22–23)

ANGER

Heartbreak can lead to serious and valid spiritual questions. It
can also push you into a confrontation with the source of life and the
authority over the universe. Let's be real: if God is truly God, and if
He is the Lord of all, there are times you have to approach Him boldly
with your raw feelings. Occasions arise when you feel compelled to
lay before Him the honest wrestling of your heart. Sometimes, that
involves outright anger. You're ticked off about what you've been
dragged through. You don't agree with what God has done, especially
when it has grieved you to the core.

Let me say up front that it is okay to be angry with God. He can
take it. God can handle your emotions as you plead with Him to
make sense of your life. God will not crumble because you're upset.
His truth will not collapse when you challenge His decisions, and His
divine plan will not be thwarted when you question His deeds. He is
a solid rock who can take the crashing waters of your hurt feelings
and the waves of your wounds and grief. Psalm 4 gives guidance for
angry sufferers: "Be angry, and do not sin; ponder in your own hearts
on your beds, and be silent. Offer right sacrifices, and put your trust
in the LORD" (vv. 4–5).

Is it possible to trust in God when you feel betrayed by Him? Di-
alogue with God means you are still depending on Him. That's what
the psalmist was saying. Even if your conversation with God is strong,
honest, and direct, you are entrusting Him with the deepest hurts of
your heart. And God will take your anger. He wants you to come to
Him when you're angry. What He doesn't want is apathy, and what

He won't accept is arrogance. God doesn't want you to disengage when you're disappointed with Him. He also doesn't want you to try to take over for Him when you feel that life isn't going your way. God calls you to connect, confront, and converse with Him when you feel snubbed and slighted. He wants you to bring your debates and complaints. His heart's desire is that you cling to His promises and call Him to account for them.

CONFRONTING AND CONNECTING

A gutsy woman did just that in Matthew 15. After Jesus spent time preaching and teaching near His hometown, He traveled to the land of Canaan, an area where pagan religions dominated and Roman rule excluded any endorsement of the true God of heaven. A woman from that region approached Jesus with loud cries and tears. She said, "Have mercy on me, O Lord, Son of David; my daughter is severely oppressed by a demon" (v. 22). Jesus didn't answer her. Then the disciples stepped in. Seeing that this woman was not at the top of the priority list for Jesus' work of outreach and salvation, they tried to send her away. But she kept shouting and pestering. Jesus said to His disciples, "I was sent only to the lost sheep of the house of Israel" (v. 24). But the woman didn't give up. She approached Jesus, knelt before Him, and said, "Lord, help me" (v. 25). Jesus replied, "It is not right to take the children's bread and throw it to the dogs" (v. 26). The frustrated and distraught woman didn't back away. She stayed engaged, even when she felt rejected. She said, "Yes, Lord, yet even the dogs eat the crumbs that fall from their masters' table" (v. 27). Jesus was moved by her tenacious trust and responded, "O woman, great is your faith! Be it done for you as you desire" (v. 28). And in that moment, the woman's daughter was healed.

A foreign woman kept hanging on to Jesus in her desperation and frustration. That is God's direction for you when you're angry with Him. He wants you to hang on to Him. When you're confronting Him with His promises, you're trusting Him. When you cry out, you're not bowing out. God wants you to bring everything you've got to Him so you can see Him work His wonders with your anger and grief.

GOD'S HEART

God knows you won't always be happy with Him. But anger isn't a taboo. Jesus received all of God's wrath as He hung on the cross. Anger over a broken, chaotic, and rebellious world was unleashed upon the Son of God as He carried the woundedness and failures of the world. In His suffering on your behalf, Jesus overcame anger. He took the sting out of it. He drained the fear from it. When He rose from the dead, He let you know that anger won't overcome anyone anymore. When your heart is broken and grief stirs your fury, you can bring it all to Jesus, confident that He knows how to handle it and what to do with it. You can bring your anger to God, knowing He won't be angry back at you. He will show His love, bring His healing, and work His miracles.

The apostle John talked about how your overwhelmed and unstable heart can receive reassurance before God. He said, "God is greater than our heart" (1 John 3:20). This is the hope you need when anger at God overwhelms you. God is greater than your anger. God is greater than your grief. He is greater than anything your heart might muster up. Don't worry. Don't be afraid. You can be angry, knowing Jesus will take it into His hands, take it off your shoulders, and walk you through it in order to help you overcome it. Jesus is the best place to go with your anger. At the right time, He will heal your heartbreak, no matter how it is expressed.

WORDS FOR HEALING

Devotion Guide for Chapter Thirty-One

READ Hebrews 5:7–9

REFLECT

Verse 7 begins by revealing the raw emotions Jesus' experienced during His life on earth. How does this encourage you?

God heard the loud cries and tears of His Son. What does this tell you about God's attitude toward you?

How do verses 8–9 instruct you about growing in character and being filled with hope?

PRAY with confidence as you bring your true emotions and feelings to God. Let Him know the promises you're holding on to. Ask Him for His help and answers.

Faith

WHEN YOU'RE WAITING FOR GOD TO ACT

[Jesus said,] "It is not for you to know times or seasons that the Father has fixed by His own authority. But you will receive power when the Holy Spirit has come upon you, and you will be My witnesses in Jerusalem and in all Judea and Samaria, and to the end of the earth." (Acts 1:7–8)

WAITING

Do you feel like your loss has placed your life on hold? Although you want to move past your heartbreak, it seems like all you do is wait. Time seems to slow down as you make your way through the long slog of shock, disappointment, and pain. Time passes as you learn the details of what happened. It takes more time to let those facts sink in and surface again as questions, feelings, and needs. In your grief, you wait as each new day brings another new adjustment and more reminders that make you sigh with sadness. You wade into the murky waters of encountering people—trying politely to answer questions about what happened and hearing words of sympathy that are kind but don't mute your heartbreak. You feel as though your life is paused, and you wonder if you will ever be able to get back to ground zero, let alone take any steps forward. You wait as the thick clouds of grief obscure what a future might look like in your new reality. Waiting, waiting, and more waiting. Will you ever be able to move forward freely again?

But let me reassure you about your time on pause. Waiting can be a holy posture. It can be a therapeutic and restoring place in the presence of God. Biblical sages lauded waiting. When adversity struck, King David shared encouraging words: "Wait for the LORD; be strong, and let your heart take courage; wait for the LORD!" (Psalm 27:14). The prophet Isaiah equated waiting for God with strength and renewal: "They who wait for the LORD shall renew their strength; they shall mount up with wings like eagles; they shall run and not be weary; they shall walk and not faint" (Isaiah 40:31).

Waiting for God doesn't mean you're squandering time or stuck on hold; it means you're being fortified and restored by the One who waits with you. The world may say waiting is a waste, but God uses waiting to grow hope. The biblical word for "wait" is interchangeable with the word for "hope." Waiting creates room for God to act and grows room in your heart to see how God shows up.

THE GIFT OF TIME

Consider how Jesus' followers were put into the position of waiting. Before Jesus ascended into heaven, His followers asked, "Lord, will You at this time restore the kingdom to Israel?" (Acts 1:6). They were ready for the completion of God's plan. They wanted everything to be all better right now. But Jesus broke the news that it was time to wait. He said, "It is not for you to know times or seasons that the Father has fixed by His own authority. But you will receive power when the Holy Spirit has come upon you, and you will be My witnesses in Jerusalem and in all Judea and Samaria, and to the end of the earth" (Acts 1:7–8). Then Jesus left them. He was lifted up into a cloud. After three years of walking together with their Master, seeing His miracles, hearing His teaching, watching Him die, and rejoicing in His resurrection, Jesus was gone. He promised He would be with them always, but physically He was no longer by their side.

So the eleven disciples walked back to Jerusalem and waited, but not with their heads hanging and not without hope. Their waiting consisted of community, prayer, and preparation. One hundred and twenty followers of Jesus gathered together to encourage one another and to pray together. Peter led the group in choosing a disciple to take Judas's place. They didn't know what was next, but they grew in stamina and readiness for whatever God had planned.

At times, making no discernible progress in your life is okay. In fact, doing nothing may be the best thing for you to do in your loss. Pausing life's frenzy of activity can honor the love and investment you poured into the precious part of your life you're now grieving. Waiting for God to act can refill your hope, restore your strength, and recalibrate your vision for the new days ahead. Remember, God said, "Be still," following that statement with "know that I am God" (Psalm

46:10). The two are intimately connected. Time may sometimes seem torturous, but in God's hands, time is grace. He uses what seem to be idle moments to meet you in the inner places of your heart. Time is God's gift to recondition your soul and reset your sights.

What happened to Jesus' followers as they waited? Pentecost arrived. What was once known as an ancient harvest festival became the birthday of the Christian Church. Silence and space gave way to the unleashing of God's Spirit and the saving of many lost lives. The waiting band of disciples became instruments in God's hand that displayed His goodness and shared God's refreshing message of hope with the world.

GOD'S HEART

If God puts you in the position of waiting, don't resist it. Stop fighting and resenting the pause you're experiencing. Instead, embrace it. Lean into waiting with prayer by resting on God's promises and drawing strength from people He has placed in your life. Wait expectantly. God makes time your friend and fills the space of waiting with His grace. Watch for His surprises. Be on the lookout for His loving care. When you find yourself waiting for God to act, you are in the treasured territory of being drawn close to Him. It's not always comfortable, and it may never be your first choice for what life would bring, but it will deepen your relationship with your Savior and lead you to be amazed at His faithful work for you. Contrary to what you might expect, waiting isn't God's way to weaken your walk with Him; it is His divine and wise strategy for strengthening you during heartbreak.

WORDS FOR HEALING
Devotion Guide for Chapter Thirty-Two

READ Psalm 130

REFLECT

How do the first two verses of this psalm reflect the struggle you're enduring right now?

What eagerness, relief, and hope can you relate to in verses 3–6?

Verses 7–8 provide a foundation for hope as you wait. What in these verses encourages and strengthens you as you wait for God to act?

PRAY expectantly, bringing your hurt, questions, and needs to God and making a commitment to wait for His response and help. Thank Him for being your refuge and strength when you feel like your life is on pause.

Faith
WHEN YOU DON'T WANT TO GO TO CHURCH

[Job said to God,] "I cry to You for help and You
do not answer me; I stand, and You only look at
me. You have turned cruel to me; with the might
of Your hand You persecute me. You lift me up on
the wind; You make me ride on it, and You toss me
about in the roar of the storm." (Job 30:20–22)

IN CROWDS

Public places can bring unpleasant ambushes during your
season of sadness. Have you felt the pressure of being with people
when you don't want to talk about your ordeal? Heartbreak is not
worked through well in public. And being in familiar places can spell
disaster for a fragile soul. One glance at the spot where you usually
sat, one whiff of that oh-so-recognizable scent, and one step into
that well-known setting can trigger a wave of anxiety and a flood of
tears. One of those familiar places may be church. The sights, the
songs, the people, the prayers—it may be too much for you.

But let's dig deeper. The environment may not be the only issue.
It may be that people seem unable to respond to you in a way that
meets your needs. They mean well, but with your heart so tender,
any inquiry can feel awkward, insensitive, or inadequate. "How are
you?" "I'm praying for you." "I know how you feel." "My cousin just
went through the same thing." Those comments can fall short. Anything said can add up to a sour experience of anger, disappointment, and sadness.

A HOME VISIT

What's the answer? You may be familiar with a man named Job.
He endured heartbreak and loss beyond the limits of what anyone
could handle. Sitting in his wounds and grief, Job said to God, "I cry
to You for help and You do not answer me; I stand, and You only look

at me. You have turned cruel to me; with the might of Your hand You persecute me. You lift me up on the wind; You make me ride on it, and You toss me about in the roar of the storm."

Job took God to task and waited for Him to respond. He challenged God to speak up. Job asked God to come to him with answers and help. Not budging from his difficult place of dust and ashes, a grieving Job invited God to meet him in his despair. Job's paralyzed spirit couldn't move. He remembered the days when he could stride into public places and be revered by both young and old as a wise and strong leader. He recalled fondly when God seemed like a close friend. But now Job didn't want to show his face in public. He felt frightened, undignified, and unsafe. He felt uncomfortable going anywhere. Job needed God to come to him. And that is what God does best.

Toward the end of the Book of Job, we hear, "Then the LORD answered Job out of the whirlwind" (38:1). God spoke up. He drew near to the broken man in need. God didn't explain every detail of His plan. He didn't give the background information about the spiritual battle that led to Job's trials. God simply came close and made Himself known.

When your feelings are too tender to allow you to come into God's presence and when you can't work up the courage to step into God's house, God is willing to visit you where you are. Home visits are His specialty. Remember that Jesus, the living Word of God, full of grace and truth, was made flesh and made His dwelling among us (John 1:14). Remember that Jesus was called "Immanuel" by the angel who foretold His birth in Matthew 1. The name means "God with us." When Jesus raised a widow's dead son back to life, the astonished crowd exclaimed, "God has visited His people!" (Luke 7:16).

The God who saves doesn't rescue from afar. He draws close to you. He walks with you. He finds you when you feel lost. He pursues you when you run away. He became just like you, feeling what you feel and able to sympathize with you as you suffer. God visits you in your sadness and leads His Church to do the same.

CHURCH ON THE MOVE

If you can't go to church, the Church can easily come to you. This involves much more than catching a worship service on television or joining an online worship opportunity from the safety of your living room. It means more than reading God's Word on your own or praying in the privacy of your home. You see, there's more to church than worship services. God didn't create the Church because we need a busy schedule of activities; He created the Church because we need each other. The Church is not just a building; it is the energetic interaction of God's redeemed community. The Church is a living and breathing organism, enlivened by the resurrection of Jesus and the sending of His Holy Spirit. God's Church consists of sent people, receiving and sharing His love and grace. It is true that God's people aren't perfect. Some may disappoint you. But God will provide others who lift you up in your times of need. He will bless you with shoulders to lean on.

So, if you feel like you can't muster up the stamina to go to church, ask the church to stop by and see you. Your pastor will be pleased to sit with you, to listen, and to pray. He will be glad to share the Lord's Supper with you. Christian friends will be overjoyed to stop by for a personal time of conversation and worship. It may be exactly what you need as you gradually and gently phase into your former routine. If you don't want to immerse yourself fully in a crowd of people, and you can't bear the thought of seeing the familiar surroundings that trigger your sadness, let a little community of trusted friends come to you so you can bring your praise and prayer to your Savior with people you trust and love. Take it slow, knowing that even if you feel far away, God is always close to you.

After He spoke to Job, God did something amazing: He restored Job completely. All the people who knew Job before his tragedies came to him "and ate bread with him in his house. . . . They showed him sympathy and comforted him" (Job 42:11). Sometimes, letting others do the visiting is exactly what you need.

WORDS FOR HEALING
Devotion Guide for Chapter Thirty-Three

READ Psalm 42:1–5

REFLECT

Verses 1–2 express a yearning for God. What makes you yearn for God's help and presence?

In verse 4, the writer remembers the wonderful days of going to church with friends, but verse 3 reflects his new reality. How has your sense of loss dampened the activities you were once able to do cheerfully?

Verse 5 is a refrain that happens three times throughout Psalms 42 and 43. How does this refrain lead you to hope and how might it become your "battle cry" as you journey through grief?

PRAY that God would draw close to you and that He would send caring people to surround you during your time of loss. Ask Him for understanding and help as you work through a season of life that sidelines you from your normal activities.

Faith
WHEN YOU THOUGHT YOU KNEW GOD'S PLAN

So Jacob served seven years for Rachel, and
they seemed to him but a few days because of
the love he had for her. (Genesis 29:20)

PLANS

Do you feel like you're standing in the wreckage of well-laid plans? You thought your life was aligned with God's will. Everything seemed to be coming together. People affirmed your direction. Your pathway seemed smooth, and your journey was going really well. It seemed so right, and for a while, it was unfolding exactly the way you hoped it would. But then the bottom dropped out. It all came crashing down. You thought you knew God's plan, but now you're absolutely confused.

I can relate to your pain. I've been in the position of being unquestionably certain that life was taking me on a clear course. God even seemed to be giving the go-ahead. But when the plan took a sharp turn off the road of my certainty, I was left absolutely bewildered. I was totally stumped, stunned, and saddened. You may be able to relate to those feelings in this moment as you ponder what seem like fouled-up plans in your life. You wonder what you're supposed to do now that everything has gone south.

THE SWITCH

Fouled-up plans make me think of Jacob. After Jacob left home to strike out on his own, he met a beautiful girl named Rachel. He fell in love with her and made a commitment to her father, Laban, that he would work seven years to earn her hand in marriage. Laban agreed. The Bible says that "Jacob served seven years for Rachel, and they seemed to him but a few days because of the love he had for her." It was a classic story of selfless romance.

What Jacob didn't know is that Laban couldn't give Rachel in marriage before her older sister Leah was married. After seven years of hard work, Leah was still single, so Laban switched every-thing. After Jacob and Rachel's wedding day was celebrated and their wedding night began, Leah was secretly sent into the bedroom to consummate the marriage. In the dark of the night, after a grand wedding celebration, Jacob had no clue that everything was about to change. Genesis 29 describes the events: "In the morning, behold, it was Leah! And Jacob said to Laban, 'What is this you have done to me? Did I not serve with you for Rachel? Why then have you de-ceived me?'" (v. 25).

There are times when you feel deceived by God. You're led to believe that the course you're taking is the one He has prepared for you. You follow it obediently and arrange your life around it. You put in time and prayer. You communicate with loved ones as the plan unfolds. You even work hard to embrace and accept where God is clearly leading you. But when the plan begins to crumble and all your hope, preparation, and expectations disintegrate with it, you're left scratching your head and asking God what in the world He is doing. You feel let down, hurt, and foolish.

THE PLAN

Here is something very important to understand: when you are convinced you know God's plan but everything changes, remember you still know God's heart. He is faithful, and He cares about you. Detours will never disconnect you from His love. Change in what you thought was certain will hurt for a time but will always give way to God's strength and restoration. You may never understand fully why your life took an undesired detour, but when your daily plans disin-tegrate, God's eternal plan for you will always endure.

Jacob's life became a wild, unexpected, and sometimes unpleas-ant journey. He was finally able to marry Rachel, but his married life became one of heartache, arguments, and bickering. Then he had to flee from a jealous and angry father-in-law. Jacob wrestled with God, bargained with his twin brother, Esau, and tolerated the squabbling of his twelve sons. He endured emotional ups and downs, fought through economic scarcity, and was uprooted from his home-land. Life was not easy for Jacob. But one component of his reality remained consistent: God never stopped speaking to him about the much larger plan for his life. After all the changes and chasing, God appeared to Jacob and blessed him. God said, "Your name is Jacob;

no longer shall your name be called Jacob, but Israel shall be your name. . . . I am God Almighty: be fruitful and multiply. A nation and a company of nations shall come from you, and kings shall come from your own body" (Genesis 35:10–11). The bigger plan for Jacob was to provide the family line of Jesus, the King of kings. God's ultimate plan was that Jacob would bless the world with the Savior of all humanity.

God's ultimate plan for you is that you will bless the world with the hope and new life He gives. His bigger plan for your life is that you will bring Jesus to a broken world. At times, that happens best when your daily plans crumble and you find yourself on your knees in prayer, calling out to God for explanations and help. It isn't that God is playing games with you. He may be protecting you or directing you where you need to go. You may never know completely. But you can be assured that depending on Him will strengthen your character, increase your compassion, and send ripples of spiritual witness and encouragement to a searching world around you. After the plans I thought were certain gave way to complete change, time helped me see God's protection and purpose. Faithful and wise friends brought counsel and clarity. And though my direction was different than I had anticipated, Jesus was faithful and gracious in the new and unexpected territory of my journey.

Has what you thought to be God's plan come crashing down? Keep traveling on the road of God's bigger plan—His eternal plan for you and the world. Stay faithful and watchful, serving others and sharing God's grace. Wait on God and walk in His ways. Instead of trying to figure everything out, trust that God will not abandon you. Have faith that He will bless you and sustain you. Know that He will, in some way, shine His bright light of hope through you. As you wander through the pain and wreckage of changed plans that confuse you, know without a doubt that God's plan of love and rescue for you—made certain by the death and resurrection of Jesus—will never change.

Words for Healing

Devotion Guide for Chapter Thirty-Four

READ Psalm 34:1–7

REFLECT

When everything changes, it is frightening to look at an uncertain future. How do verses 1–4 help you in your fear?

When you think you know God's plan and those plans take a detour, you can feel foolish. What do verses 5–6 tell you about God's care when your emotions are left hanging?

How does the imagery in verse 7 encourage you during your times of uncertainty?

PRAY that God would encamp around you as you journey through your fragile time of heartbreak. Let Him know your biggest questions. Ask Him to guide you with His Word of grace and truth.

People
WHEN PEOPLE SEEM TO JUDGE YOU

Now the birth of Jesus Christ took place in this way.
When His mother Mary had been betrothed to Joseph,
before they came together she was found to be with
child from the Holy Spirit. And her husband Joseph,
being a just man and unwilling to put her to shame,
resolved to divorce her quietly. (Matthew 1:18–19)

JUDGMENT

Do you ever feel judged because you've experienced heartbreak? It hurts, doesn't it? When you are in the middle of loss, there are times when people will issue a decree of condemnation and send it your way. The decree will insinuate you are to blame and interrogate you with questions: "What did you do to cause this situation? Why didn't you take action sooner? Did you make the best decisions you could have in your circumstances? Couldn't you recognize the pitfalls and hazards ahead of time?"

It is hurtful to be accused of irresponsibility and faulted for ignorance when you are suffering grief and pain. Of course, sometimes you accuse yourself. Some of the judgment you feel may be self-imposed. Your inner voice may be whispering, "People must think you're completely incompetent. You look foolish. Why are you so pathetic?"

Whether you're feeling condemnation from yourself or the people around you, judgment is always crushing. It is the last thing you need when you are enduring heart-wrenching loss. Honestly, in your heart of hearts, you may know that some of the accusations are true. You may have dropped the ball. You may have failed. Maybe you should have seen what was coming. Perhaps you should have taken action in a more timely way. But at the time, you didn't know. Hindsight is twenty-twenty, and there is no way you can undo your pain, but you certainly do not need meanness and judgment at a time like this. Having the sting of condemnation sent your way aggravates your pain and deepens your hurt. Criticism wears you down and sends you into a deeper and lonelier wilderness.

REDIRECTION

A man named Joseph tossed and turned with weariness and worry as he felt the wounds of judgment in his life. He was engaged to a girl named Mary, who revealed to him that she was pregnant—not by him, but by the Holy Spirit. The tale seemed too bizarre to believe. Joseph was a righteous man, a dignified follower of God's ways. He was a leader in the community. What would people say about this? What would they say about him? And what would they do to the girl he loved? Joseph expected a judgmental and cruel response. According to the law, Mary could have deserved death for what appeared to everyone to be unfaithfulness. The pressure pushed Joseph into a decision. Matthew 1 says that "Joseph, being a just man and unwilling to put her to shame, resolved to divorce her quietly." Then, with his mind and heart overloaded with sadness and fear, Joseph fell asleep. That's when God stepped in and changed everything.

When judgment and condemnation make you weary, God reveals His counterintuitive grace. You may see no way out, and the burden on your shoulders may make you feel as if you can never stand under its weight, but God is good at showing you that help and freedom are much closer than you think.

As Joseph slept, an angel of the Lord appeared to him in a dream and said, "Joseph, son of David, do not fear to take Mary as your wife, for that which is conceived in her is from the Holy Spirit. She will bear a son, and you shall call His name Jesus, for He will save His people from their sins" (Matthew 1:20–21). God turned judgment inside out. He removed condemnation and let Joseph know that the perplexing events of his life were part of a perfect plan. With a word, God corrected Joseph's course and restored Joseph's heart.

Sometimes, judgment pushes you away from walking with God and tempts you to fall into the trap of figuring out a plan of your own. You become self-conscious, guilt-ridden, and desperate for relief. You begin to cave in to the critique of people who have no idea what you've been going through. You end up beating yourself up and descending into despair. That's when you need God's gracious redirection. Even if you were wrong all along, God's Word says to you,

"There is therefore now no condemnation for those who are in Christ Jesus" (Romans 8:1). Even if you made some mistakes and acted foolishly, God's Word speaks into your weariness and says, "Who shall bring any charge against God's elect? It is God who justifies. Who is to condemn? Christ Jesus is the one who died—more than that, who was raised—who is at the right hand of God, who indeed is interceding for us" (Romans 8:33–34).

When judgment tries to win the day and crush your heart, Jesus speaks up with a verdict of "not guilty!" He intercedes for you as the One who took your judgment upon Himself when He was put to death and destroyed your condemnation when He rose to life again. The antidote to judgment is Jesus. The answer for condemnation is Christ's call out of the wilderness of public opinion and self-loathing. And take heart, Jesus is always closer than you think. With one whisper of His Word in your weariness, He will redirect you to His life-giving grace and truth.

A NEW WAY

You see why it is so important to read and hear God's Word. It is powerful and life restoring. It speaks to your deepest needs and drowns out the noise of a condemning world. It is filled with God's love and drains away the mean and unsympathetic static of people who don't know what they're talking about. It also helps fill you with compassion, so you can love others as God first loved you. Instead of getting caught up in a chain reaction of condemnation, you can break that chain of judgment with a heart and life filled with Jesus' unconditional love.

That's what happened to Joseph. He woke up and did exactly what the angel of the Lord commanded him. Living against the flow of a critical world, he took Mary as his wife, celebrated the birth of her baby boy, named Him Jesus, and understood that God's wise ways would bring life to a broken world. Living in God's love will always stop condemnation in its tracks.

WORDS FOR HEALING
Devotion Guide for Chapter Thirty-Five

READ Psalm 54

REFLECT

This psalm is a prayer that asks for vindication in the face of unfair judgment. How do the first three verses capture your feelings as you face people's condemnation?

How do verses 4–5 show you God's faithfulness in your life?

Verses 6–7 give a commitment of thanksgiving to God. How do you show gratitude to God for His kindness and pay His compassion forward to others?

PRAY for strength as you endure unfair judgment. Ask God to give you confidence in His unconditional love.

People
WHEN NOBODY LISTENS TO YOU

Then [Jesus] went home, and the crowd gathered again,
so that they could not even eat. And when His family
heard it, they went out to seize Him, for they were
saying, "He is out of His mind." (Mark 3:20–21)

IS ANYONE LISTENING?

Listening seems to be a lost art these days, doesn't it? Distraction is at a high point. Noise and multitasking seem to be the norm. Do you ever wonder if anyone really hears you? If someone does give you the chance to unload some of your heartbreak, chances are high that you will end up listening to the story of his life or hearing how her aunt or cousin or friend went through the exact same thing you're enduring—only worse.

I remember learning about something called "reflective listening." It involved the discipline to reflect back what a person was telling you by asking probing questions. If a person said she had a wonderful vacation, reflective listening would keep you from responding, "That's great! I had a fantastic getaway too. Let me tell you all about my vacation." Instead of turning the conversation back on yourself, you would turn it back to the person who is sharing. You would say things like this: "Tell me about it. What was your favorite experience? What would make you want to go again?"

Reflective listening is a discipline, because our tendency is not to listen at all. By default, we think about ourselves. Our reflex is to turn the conversation into talking about me, me, me. We don't think about the value of truly understanding someone else, and we don't like the silent gaps in conversation when we make the commitment to let someone else process his or her thoughts and feelings. That's why it's so difficult to find someone who will take an interest in your grief and hear you out during your heartbreak.

Jesus understood this predicament. Interestingly enough, Jesus was one of the most ignored people in history. People's personal agendas constantly got in the way of hearing His Good News that God had come close to help His people. Even His own disciples descended into arguments about who among them was the greatest instead of paying rapt attention to Jesus' words of wisdom and insight. His own followers drifted to sleep instead of being attentive to His needs of support and prayer.

There are so many agendas out there. And those needs, thoughts, plans, and desires create barriers to hearing one another. Is it possible, then, for anyone to listen to you? Is anyone available emotionally to be attentive to the deep questions of your heart and to receive the feelings you need to express? The truth is, you may have to help them. You may have to give some tips and do some preparation—even with trusted friends and loved ones. You may have to preface your sharing with prompts: "I don't want you to solve this or fix it; I just need you to listen. Please hear me out and be in the moment with me. I'm going to vent for a little while; could you just hear what I have to say and not interrupt until I tell you I'm finished?"

It would be wonderful if you didn't have to go to all this effort, but even the Son of God had to recondition His hearers. There was a time when Jesus was teaching in a local house. So many people gathered and the demand from Him was so great that He and His disciples weren't even able to stop and eat. That's when people around Jesus started to tune Him out. Mark 3 tells us, "When [Jesus'] family heard it, they went out to seize Him, for they were saying, 'He is out of His mind.' And the scribes who came down from Jerusalem were saying, 'He is possessed by Beelzebul,' and 'by the prince of demons He casts out the demons' " (vv. 21–22). No one was really listening. Jesus' own family and His fellow church members made assumptions that got in the way of hearing and understanding Him. So Jesus said to them, "How can Satan cast out Satan? If a kingdom is divided against itself, that kingdom cannot stand" (vv. 23–24).

Jesus recalibrated their thinking and did His best to open their hearts and ears to hear Him. He also showed you that, sometimes, the people closest to you have the hardest time hearing you. They care about you so much that they become afraid of losing you in your hurt.

THE ULTIMATE LISTENER

That's why it is important to know that God provides listeners in your life. You may know one or two people who are truly attentive to you. You may be blessed with a friend or loved one who is really good at listening. But you also may need to speak with a trusted counselor who can listen without fear and offer input in a caring and objective way. It's okay to seek refuge from the world's noise by sitting at the feet of a professional who is attentive to the needs of your heart. The Bible calls us to "bear one another's burdens" (Galatians 6:2). As a loved one or counselor listens well, God is not only providing you with an outlet for your grief, but He is also conditioning your heart so you can be a listener for others who are suffering loss.

God also provides Himself as the ultimate listener. He gives you the gift of prayer. Because Jesus can completely sympathize with you, God's Word says, "Let us then with confidence draw near to the throne of grace, that we may receive mercy and find grace to help in time of need" (Hebrews 4:16). You will always find the help you need in the attentive and listening ear of your Savior. You can pour out your heart to Him with confidence and boldness. After God made the commitment to give His beloved people a hope and a future, He added an important promise for every person who is heartbroken: "Then you will call upon Me and come and pray to Me, and I will hear you" (Jeremiah 29:12). Prayer is God's open door of dependable and sympathetic listening. Sometimes, people wonder why God seems so silent. Perhaps it's because He is such a good listener.

Be assured, Jesus is not afraid of your feelings. He is not threatened by your rants. He is not shaken by your doubts. Jesus can listen to you with deep understanding and compassion because He has been where you are. He will hear you and will help you.

WORDS FOR HEALING

Devotion Guide for Chapter Thirty-Six

READ Psalm 17:6–8

REFLECT

The writer of this psalm, King David, expressed complete confidence that God would hear him. What value do you find in the fact that God truly listens to what you say?

How have you seen God show His steadfast love to you as you navigate grief and loss?

Verse 8 provides powerful imagery about God's care for you. What does it mean to be the apple of His eye and to be hidden in the shadow of His wings?

PRAY that God will hear you, that He will protect you, and that He will strengthen you. Ask Him to provide faithful listeners in your life who will show you sympathy and help ease your burden.

People
WHEN YOUR FRIENDS SAY THEY UNDERSTAND

Now when Job's three friends heard of all this evil that
had come upon him, they came each from his own place,
Eliphaz the Temanite, Bildad the Shuhite, and Zophar
the Naamathite. They made an appointment together to
come to show him sympathy and comfort him. (Job 2:11)

FRIENDS

Friends are precious gifts. True friends are rare treasures. People
who understand you, listen to you, love you, walk with you through
the highs and lows of life, and are bold enough to hold you account-
able are special blessings from God and are not easily found. But
friends are not perfect, and not every person in your life is able to be
the friend you need when you endure heartbreak.

Our world has a low tolerance for pain, so when you encounter
grief, you will tend to find more people who want you to get through
it quickly rather than journey with you through it gradually. You'll
discover people who want to explain your problem, fix your problem,
and tell you how to get over your problem. They mean well; they care.
But you know that being rushed through a matter of your heart is
not helpful. You need someone who is willing to wait with you as you
process your loss—even if it means waiting a lifetime. In a short-
term, quick-fix world, you need long-haul people who are willing to
endure what may be an endless journey. You need friends who are
committed to loving you at your lowest point.

THE FRIEND

There may be a person in your life who can do that. Someone
who can walk the long road of unconditional love and support may
be present for you. But there are crowds of people who are not in
that place. They're not defective friends, and they are not at fault for
carelessness. They just don't have that kind of relationship with you.

The Book of Proverbs offers wisdom about friendship when it says, "A man of many companions may come to ruin, but there is a friend who sticks closer than a brother" (Proverbs 18:24).

The verse highlights that you may have many companions. Your Facebook list of friends may be large. You may have a pile of followers on Pinterest. You may be surrounded by crowds of people at work. But that doesn't mean they are able to step up as the friend you need in your heartbreak. Please don't blame them, write them off, or become angry with them. They simply highlight your need for the "friend who sticks closer than a brother."

It's no accident that Jesus said to His followers, "I have called you friends" (John 15:15). He also expresses that precious sentiment to you as you walk in faith. You are not just a name on Jesus' church membership list. You're not merely a face in the crowd of Christ's believers. You're not an imperfect and needy burden Jesus has to lug through life. You are Jesus' friend. "Greater love has no one than this," Jesus said, "that someone lay down his life for his friends" (John 15:13). Jesus proved His bond of friendship with you by doing just that. He died for you, not because you were so noble, but because you were so needy. Jesus loved you at your lowest point, and He is alive to continue loving you during your deepest need. Jesus is your true friend who understands you and walks patiently with you. Your Savior not only understands the grief you can express, but He also understands your groans too deep for words. Jesus doesn't rush you through your pain; He rushes to you and stays with you.

HELPING HEARERS

As fallen people, we're a different story. Don't be too surprised when your friends say they understand but don't really get it. It happened to a man named Job as he suffered horrible loss. The Bible tells us that Job's friends, Eliphaz, Bildad, and Zophar, came to show him sympathy and give him comfort. They started out fairly well. They wept with him, sat with him, and didn't say a word. For a while they abided by the wisdom of someone who said, "Don't just do something; stand there." They were present for a suffering friend. It's wonderful when people are there for you. But then Job's friends decided to speak up. Thinking they understood exactly what was happening, they slid down the slippery slope of trying to explain Job's heartbreak, telling him to get over it and trying to fix it. What was Job's reply? When Eliphaz blamed Job for his trouble, Job said, "My brothers are treacherous as a torrent-bed" (Job 6:15). When Bildad told Job to be done with his sulking, Job responded, "If I say, 'I will forget my complaint, I will put off my sad face, and be of good cheer,' I become afraid of all my suffering" (Job 9:27–28). When Zophar gave advice to fix Job's pain, Job shot back, "Worthless physicians are you all" (Job 13:4).

Job didn't take kindly to friends who didn't understand. He didn't need to hear explanations, brush-offs, or advice to help him get over his grief. He needed friends to be there, to grieve with him, and to show him compassion.

God is that kind of friend to you, and He teaches you to be that kind of friend to others. The apostle Paul said it well when he spoke about the "God of all comfort, who comforts us in all our affliction, so that we may be able to comfort those who are in any affliction, with the comfort with which we ourselves are comforted by God" (2 Corinthians 1:3–4). That's a mouthful, but it's a mouthful with great meaning. God is the God of all comfort who transforms you into a person of true comfort. Finding a friend who understands you may start with being a friend who is truly understanding.

So, give some grace to your friends who sometimes fumble. You can show them understanding and compassion because you are leaning on the friend you have in Jesus.

WORDS FOR HEALING

Devotion Guide for Chapter Thirty-Seven

READ Psalm 71:17–21

REFLECT

Verses 17–18 tell of God's long-term presence and His commitment throughout your life. What good things can you tell others about His dependable friendship?

God is with you during your highs and lows. More than that, He keeps you steady, revives you, and comforts you. How do verses 19–21 give you hope?

What comfort from your friend Jesus do you need most during this time of your life?

PRAY for God's understanding to overflow into bringing you the comfort you need. Let God know where you are hurt and how you feel alone. Ask Him to walk closely with you and to fill you with hope and peace.

Future

WHEN YOU DREAD HAVING TO FACE ANOTHER DAY

The steadfast love of the LORD never ceases; His
mercies never come to an end. (Lamentations 3:22)

NIGHT

Loss takes away more than what your heart held precious. It also
robs you of your normal routines and the dependability of your daily
comforts. You toss and turn at night. You lose your appetite. Your
ambition slips away. Your ability to focus falters. You don't want to
talk to anybody. You don't even want to get dressed in the morning.
Heartbreak can lead you to dread having to face another day.

This deep valley of despair cuts you off from any desire for the
future. You can't see any hope ahead as your sadness overwhelms
you, and you have no desire for a future as you grieve your loss. Why
go on when you have so much less to live for? Why would you want to
consider the days ahead when a big reason for your life is now gone?
Even if you resolve to plod forward, how will you find any energy—
let alone enthusiasm—to forge into loneliness and loss?

A LIMITED LOOK

During times when you dread facing another day, it is important to get perspective on your ability to see the future. The apostle
Paul said, "Now we see in a mirror dimly, but then face to face. Now
I know in part; then I shall know fully" (1 Corinthians 13:12). The
"now" is today—this broken, imperfect, limited, and hurt-filled life.
The "then" is when Jesus returns and restores all things. Our view
now is comparable to looking through a pea-soup fog. You may be
able to see the immediate area around you, but it's impossible to see
anything ahead of you. When Jesus returns, you will gain remarkable perspective. You'll understand what and why and how. There will
come a day when everything makes sense. But for now, the mirror is
dim and cloudy.

That's why God comes to help. Great distress is always met by

God with greater hope. Jesus said it well: "In the world you will have tribulation. But take heart; I have overcome the world" (John 16:33). King David articulated that point and counterpoint, as well. He declared, "God is our refuge and strength, a very present help in trouble" (Psalm 46:1). Trouble always comes to our broken lives in this fallen world, but God is our help and fortress.

When you dread having to face another day, you don't have to face it alone. God faces each day for you, and He will fill each one with His grace, strength, and hope.

LAMENTATIONS

Jeremiah endured the life-sapping struggle of loss that drained away any desire to think about tomorrow. He witnessed the destruction of Jerusalem, the death of his countrymen, and the disgrace of people he held precious. His grief is expressed in the beautiful poetic Book of Lamentations. Five poems of lament capture Jeremiah's heartbreak and pain. The Hebrew name for the book is "How!" It is the haunting first word of exclamation that expresses pain and abandonment: "How the city sits alone!" This book of the Bible is read aloud regularly at the Wailing Wall in Jerusalem today. The outcries of pain reflect the profound woundedness of anyone experiencing loss.

You may be able to relate to Jeremiah's pained words: "Judah has gone into exile because of affliction and hard servitude; she dwells now among the nations, but finds no resting place; her pursuers have all overtaken her in the midst of her distress" (Lamentations 1:3). "For these things I weep; my eyes flow with tears; for a comforter is far from me, one to revive my spirit" (Lamentations 1:16). "My eyes are spent with weeping; my stomach churns" (Lamentations 2:11). "What can I say for you, to what compare you, O daughter of Jerusalem? . . . For your ruin is vast as the sea; who can heal you?" (Lamentations 2:13).

The weeping prophet could find no comfort in his present reality. Today was a disaster, a reason for mourning and tears. Tomorrow appeared to offer no hope and no appeal. But God surprised this broken messenger. Smack-dab in the middle of Lamentations is an astounding section of statements that reinforce this truism: "It is not what the future holds, but who holds the future." Jeremiah said, "But this

I call to mind, and therefore I have hope: The steadfast love of the LORD never ceases; His mercies never come to an end; they are new every morning; great is Your faithfulness. 'The LORD is my portion,' says my soul, 'therefore I will hope in Him' " (Lamentations 3:21–24).

HOPE FOR THE FUTURE

When the thought of tomorrow fills you with dread and makes you weary, you can put tomorrow where it belongs—in God's caring hands. Jesus said, "Do not be anxious about tomorrow, for tomorrow will be anxious for itself" (Matthew 6:34). Jesus was letting you know that you do not have to carry the burden of the future; He's carrying that on His shoulders for you. You can focus on today, knowing God's great mercy is new every morning and His faithfulness will not fail.

If the dread of another day wells up in your soul, God gives you His promise to sustain you. The ultimate future, God assures, is one where He will wipe every tear from your eyes and where there will be no more death or mourning or crying or pain (Revelation 21:4). That is what tomorrow holds. That's why you can rest in God's hope today.

Even Jeremiah said, "I called on Your name, O LORD, from the depths of the pit; You heard my plea, 'Do not close Your ear to my cry for help!' You came near when I called on You; You said, 'Do not fear!' " (Lamentations 3:55–57).

Today, don't be afraid. Today is a day when God will walk with you and show you His faithful help, one step, one moment, and one breath at a time. Today you can collapse into God's strong arms and let Him carry you. Today you can cry out to Him and know He hears you. Today, you don't have to worry. Just breathe. Jesus will shoulder your heartbreak and bring you new mercies for every tomorrow.

WORDS FOR HEALING
Devotion Guide for Chapter Thirty-Eight

READ Psalm 118:22–29

REFLECT

Verse 22 is quoted in the Gospels by Jesus as a reference to His suffering and saving work. How does this prophetic reference help give you confidence about your future?

How do the words of verses 23–24 condition your heart and soul to face each day?

What confidence do verses 25–29 express as you deal with your heartbreak and grief?

PRAY verse 24 about today. Ask God to show you why you can rejoice even in your struggle. Tell Him your worries about the future, and let Him know you trust Him with the days ahead.

Future

WHEN YOU NEED HOPE

I, John, your brother and partner in the tribulation and the kingdom and the patient endurance that are in Jesus, was on the island called Patmos on account of the word of God and the testimony of Jesus. I was in the Spirit on the Lord's day, and I heard behind me a loud voice like a trumpet. (Revelation 1:9–10)

DESPERATE NEED

Heartbreak can be like a prison sentence that has no release date. You sit in the stark confines of sadness with nothing that helps you believe life will be okay again. The cold and gray surroundings of your loss create only greater fear that you will be in this unpleasant and sorrowful place forever.

Grief can be like a long journey that keeps you asking, "Are we there yet?" No mile markers show your progress, and no rest areas come along to relieve your dread or doubt. As far as you know, the journey will never end and the ultimate destination holds no excitement or joy.

As you travel the wearying pilgrimage of pain and loss, you need something to sustain you. You need a glimmer, some grace, a respite, some rest. You need hope.

Grief doesn't come with a built-in bright side or with a steady set of positives to outweigh the oppressive negatives. Living through loss is thick and dense, harsh and sad. It grants no mercy and provides no reprieves. The only help possible must break in from the outside. You know that you can't fight your way out of heartbreak. It's impossible to plot your way out of the confines of sadness. No matter how smart or strong you are, you need external aid to extricate you from your pain.

HOPE SHOWS UP

The apostle John experienced that freeing and surprising intervention. He was in a literal prison on the island of Patmos, exiled because of his proclamation of Jesus in the hostile environment of first-century Rome. Away from his loved ones and confined to a cave, the elderly John may have thought all was lost. As far as he knew, he could very well languish in that lonely place until he died. There was no end in sight, no encouragement in view. So, one Sunday, as was his practice, John spent time in worship and prayer. Even in his loneliness and loss, John poured out his soul to God.

That's important for all of us to learn. When life doesn't feel good and all looks lost, the best course of action is to look to Jesus, who seeks and saves the lost. John knew what Jesus was able to do. As an apostle, John had seen Jesus' miracles, heard Jesus' teaching, sat stunned during Jesus' transfiguration, wept over Jesus' crucifixion, and marveled at Jesus' resurrection. There was truly nothing impossible for the living Son of God. When life appears to be at a dead end, and you can imagine no solution to your struggle, give God what He wants: a chance with your challenge. You should never keep your impossibilities to yourself. God rejoices when you take refuge in Him.

On that day, as John was in the Spirit, he heard a loud voice speak to him. The voice was overwhelming, he said, as loud and majestic as a trumpet and as full and dominating as the roar of rushing waters. John turned to see who was speaking, and he saw someone he knew. There before him was the majestic Son of God—Jesus in all His glory. Hope had just shown up.

YOU WILL NOT BE DISAPPOINTED

This may be the most important lifeline you have during your time of loss; it could very well be the most essential reality for you to understand as you navigate heartbreak: hope will not disappoint you when you hope in Jesus, your Savior.

The apostle Paul lived that reality and expressed that identical truth. He said, "We rejoice in our sufferings, knowing that suffering produces endurance, and endurance produces character, and character produces hope, and hope does not put us to shame, because God's love has been poured into our hearts through the Holy Spirit who has been given to us" (Romans 5:3–5). Just as the God of hope was present with John through the appearance of the living Christ, the God of hope is present in your life through the gift of the Holy Spirit. And the Holy Spirit is located in clear and identifiable places. Through God's Word, the Holy Spirit speaks to bring you life-transforming and eternal hope. In Baptism, the Holy Spirit enters your life to fill you with the hope of forgiveness and salvation. God's love is poured into your heart as the Spirit makes His way into your life.

No matter what prison you feel like you're in, and regardless of what interminable journey you feel like you're traveling, God is sending hope into your life right now through His living Word and certain presence. For life's difficult trek, the apostle Paul assured you of God's attentive company. Paul said, "If while we were enemies we were reconciled to God by the death of His Son, much more, now that we are reconciled, shall we be saved by His life" (Romans 5:10). In Jesus Christ, God rescued you for eternity, but He also reaches into your day-to-day life with His grace and care. As you walk by faith in God, watch for hope to show up every step of the way.

HOPE FOR THE FUTURE

In the mysterious Book of Revelation, the apostle John shared his encouraging vision with persecuted and suffering followers of Jesus. God went to great lengths to provide a glimpse of His faithful action of protection and advocacy behind the scenes of what appeared to be a dominant and faith-crushing culture. John and his listeners desperately needed hope. And hope showed up. When you need real hope, don't reach into the reservoir of your own dwindling resources; receive Him who is our hope, Jesus Christ (1 Timothy 1:1). Watch and see. Jesus brings light to the darkness. He brings encouragement to the discouraged. He speaks into your sadness and lifts you up in your loss. Jesus will always bring the hope you need.

WORDS FOR HEALING

Devotion Guide for Chapter Thirty-Nine

READ Psalm 33:16–22

REFLECT

How do verses 16–17 clarify the reality of trusting in our own strength and abilities?

What promises stand out to you and encourage you in verses 18–19?

How do verses 20–22 chart a course for your walk of faith?

PRAY for God's hope to be present in your life. Ask Him to encourage you in your weakness and to lift you up in your sadness. Let God know why you need His hope today. Let Him know you'll be watching and listening for His encouragement.

Future

WHEN YOU'RE READY FOR ETERNITY

For to me to live is Christ, and to die
is gain. (Philippians 1:21)

AWAY FROM HOME

There's nothing wrong with being ready for heaven. When you compare perfect bliss with the maddening brokenness of this world, paradise looks very good. When you find yourself in the wreckage and weariness of grief, complete restoration and comfort become very appealing. Heaven is a very good place. It is home—an unblemished place of rest and fulfillment crafted by Jesus who gave His life for you. It is the promised destination as you walk with Jesus in the newness of life. But if you're not there yet, then God wants you to be here. If Jesus hasn't called you to heaven, He still has a plan for you here on earth. That means, when the going gets tough here and now, you need a strategy to sustain you.

God willingly and intentionally gives you rest and replenishment along life's journey. But as you experience difficult times, you can be certain that He doesn't keep you on earth to make you squirm in meaninglessness. He doesn't give you life so you can be purposeless and aimless. God cherishes your life and uses every moment of your existence to contribute to His caring plan of salvation. That includes your heartbreak.

When adversity hits, you may feel like fleeing. You want to escape the sadness and pain. You want to avoid the discomfort and despair. If you were given a lofty reason for your struggle and a timeline for your grief, you could jump in with both feet, obediently tough it out, and move on with life when it is finished. But that's not the way heartbreak works. Loss swoops in as a surprise. Grief shocks you with its emptiness and tears. There is no owner's manual or contract. Suddenly, life isn't very good. And you may want out.

WEAKNESS AND GRACE

That is why it is so important to hear from someone who walked this path well and charted this course with God's wisdom. The apostle Paul yearned for heavenly restoration. Over and over again, he suffered pain and loss. In 2 Corinthians 12, he spoke about what he called his "thorn in the flesh." We don't know exactly what this malady was, but it made Paul miserable and pushed him to the edge of complete despair. Three times he pleaded with God to take away this terrible source of suffering. But God told him, "My grace is sufficient for you, for My power is made perfect in weakness" (2 Corinthians 12:9). Paul responded, "Therefore I will boast all the more gladly of my weaknesses, so that the power of Christ may rest upon me. For the sake of Christ, then, I am content with weaknesses, insults, hardships, persecutions, and calamities. For when I am weak, then I am strong" (2 Corinthians 12:9–10).

When loss lays you low, you can learn an important lesson from Paul: your greatest strength will be found in your most wearying weakness because that is when you become dependent on God's grace alone. Throughout his writings, Paul spoke to world-weary souls. He confessed his personal weakness and the perseverance he received by God's grace when he said, "We are afflicted in every way, but not crushed; perplexed, but not driven to despair; persecuted, but not forsaken; struck down, but not destroyed; always carrying in the body the death of Jesus, so that the life of Jesus may also be manifested in our bodies" (2 Corinthians 4:8–10).

PURPOSE HERE AND THERE

Paul always kept an eye on heaven but saw important purpose in his journey on earth. He said, "So we do not lose heart. Though our outer self is wasting away, our inner self is being renewed day by day. For this light momentary affliction is preparing for us an eternal weight of glory beyond all comparison" (2 Corinthians 4:16–17). He added, "We would rather be away from the body and at home with the Lord. So whether we are at home or away, we make it our aim to please Him" (2 Corinthians 5:8–9).

This is the delicate balance you experience as you endure suffering and loss. Both life in heaven and life on earth are life in the restoring and renewing Christ. That is why Paul said, "Christ will be honored in my body, whether by life or by death. For to me to live is Christ, and to die is gain" (Philippians 1:20–21). The apostle yearned for eternity but continued to serve His Savior through every twist and turn here and now.

God has an important reason for you to be here. You may never know it fully, and at times, it may feel very unpleasant, but you are an irreplaceable part of His plan. Even in your heartbreak—especially in your heartbreak—He will shine His grace through you to people and a world in need.

YOUR PATHWAY AHEAD

What is your calling when you're ready for eternity? Paul said it best: to press on. He spoke with faith and courage in Philippians 3: "Not that I have already obtained [the resurrection from the dead] or am already perfect, but I press on to make it my own, because Christ Jesus has made me His own. Brothers, I do not consider that I have made it my own. But one thing I do: forgetting what lies behind and straining forward to what lies ahead, I press on toward the goal for the prize of the upward call of God in Christ Jesus" (vv. 12–14).

Press on. You have received the gift of eternal life by faith in Jesus Christ. The life you live does not dead-end in death; by God's grace, it keeps going with the uninterrupted presence and blessing of Jesus. Your days of sadness may feel trying and torturous. You may believe your time here and now is a waste, but the hope of heaven transforms your purpose this side of paradise. Hear Paul once again: "Our citizenship is in heaven, and from it we await a Savior, the Lord Jesus Christ, who will transform our lowly body to be like His glorious body, by the power that enables Him even to subject all things to Himself. Therefore, my brothers, whom I love and long for, my joy and crown, stand firm thus in the Lord, my beloved" (Philippians 3:20–4:1).

When you're ready for eternity, press on and stand firm. God's grace will shine through you and, in His time, God's grace will bring you home.

WORDS FOR HEALING
Devotion Guide for Chapter Forty

READ Psalm 16

REFLECT

How do verses 1–6 encourage you in continuing your walk with God even as you face the challenge of loss?

What do verses 7–8 tell you about your need for God's Word and strength?

Verses 9–11 provide the hope of heaven and strength for life on earth. How do these verses help you press on and stand firm?

PRAY for endurance as you live life this side of heaven. Ask God to sustain you as you wait for your complete restoration.

Future

WHEN YOU DON'T KNOW YOUR PURPOSE ANYMORE

They heard the sound of the LORD God walking in the garden in the cool of the day, and the man and his wife hid themselves from the presence of the LORD God among the trees of the garden. But the LORD God called to the man and said to him, "Where are you?" (Genesis 3:8–9)

NOW WHAT?

When your life takes an unexpected turn after you thought you knew where you were going, you find yourself asking big questions about your purpose. What do you do now? What's next? Can you find meaning and purpose in life again?

In your loss, you may face a vast void. The love you showed, the care you gave, the efforts you made, and the commitment you embraced may not seem to matter anymore. There was no phase-out plan and no orderly transition. You weren't preparing for a radical change in your life—at least not one this drastic and bewildering. You were looking forward to a longer connection and unbroken continuity. Growth was on the horizon. You hoped and planned for a flourishing and developing venture that would bring fulfillment and focus. A complete stop and total halt never came to mind.

Now you ask, "Why am I here?"

DYNAMIC POSITIONING

The answer to that question is not something you can hurry. You've set sail on a new journey. You don't know what lies ahead, and you have serious questions about whether you will discover the shores of a new plan and purpose. But on this expedition, God steps in with grace and guidance.

The captain of a ship recently told me about his vessel's dynamic positioning system. When the ship stopped offshore to ferry some passengers to a port, I noticed that the ship's anchor wasn't used. The captain explained that the ship was equipped with satellite technology, sensors, and compass systems that operated its thrusters and propellers in order to keep the ship exactly where it needed to be and to direct it where it needed to go. This amazing technological innovation saves the reefs and provides confidence for the voyage.

As the wind and waves of life try to toss you about, the dynamic positioning system of God's Word and promise brings you the stability you need. God outlined His supernatural plan and promise to a group of uncertain exiles displaced from Jerusalem:

> For I know the plans I have for you, declares the LORD, plans for welfare and not for evil, to give you a future and a hope. Then you will call upon Me and come and pray to Me, and I will hear you. You will seek Me and find Me, when you seek Me with all your heart. I will be found by you, declares the LORD, and I will restore your fortunes and gather you from all the nations and all the places where I have driven you, declares the LORD, and I will bring you back to the place from which I sent you into exile. (Jeremiah 29:11–14)

God directed a fearful and confused group of people to seek Him, trust Him, and call upon Him. He promised to hear them, be present for them, and restore them. As you embark on discovering your new purpose, God provides His stabilizing and guiding grace. You may not know exactly where you are going, but you're given the blessing of calling upon and seeking refuge in the One who does. You may not know how your life will come together, but you can trust that you are God's precious child and that He delights in restoring you. Your Savior will always bring you back from the exile of sadness and loss. He will also direct you to a place of holy purpose.

Jesus pointed the way when He said, "You are the light of the world. A city set on a hill cannot be hidden. Nor do people light a lamp and put it under a basket, but on a stand, and it gives light to all in the house. In the same way, let your light shine before others, so that they may see your good works and give glory to your Father who is in heaven" (Matthew 5:14–16).

The truth is, you have an irreplaceable purpose even though you can't always see it or understand it. As you wait for more answers and direction, you can be confident that God will use your life to shine His love to the people around you—even when you don't realize it is happening.

DISCOVERING YOUR PURPOSE

Adam and Eve faced a crisis of purpose after they disobeyed God by eating the forbidden fruit in the Garden of Eden. After they took their future into their own hands, they were left with loss and sadness. Instead of walking with God, they hid from Him. So God pursued them. As He walked in the garden, He called out to His beloved people, "Where are you?"

The question was referring not only to their hiding place, but it also made reference to their lostness now that they had walked away from God. But even after this heartbreak, God's dynamic positioning kicked in. First, He promised that they would be the source of salvation for the world. Jesus would come from their family. This yet-to-be-born Savior would crush the power of sin forever. Second, God sent them from the garden to share the promise of salvation with all the people who would come after them. Adam and Eve, who stumbled into darkness, would be God's light for the world.

Your circumstances may make you feel worthless, but God always gives you a grand purpose: to be loved by Him and to let that love bring hope to the world. No matter what loss you are experiencing, you are on a journey, by God's grace, to fulfill His purpose. You may not fully understand what that purpose is, and you may see only occasional glimpses of your reason for being, but you can trust that God is doing something of critical importance with your life—even if you can't make sense of it.

In the emptiness and perplexity of loss, you are placed into the position of giving God room to act. It is healthy to have space in your life for God to fill in the blanks, to open new doors of opportunity, and to grow passion in your heart for new ventures. You don't need to hurry. There is no pressure to rush into activity and become busy with many things. Filling your day in order to forget about your loss may crowd out God's whispers and direction for your future. Busyness may obscure what God is beginning to build right in front of your eyes. With the dynamic positioning God provides, you can wait confidently for Him. You can trust that He knows you, hears you, loves you, and will provide all you need.

WORDS FOR HEALING

Devotion Guide for Chapter Forty-One

READ Psalm 147:1–11

REFLECT

In what way do verses 1–3 give you encouragement during your time of "exile"?

How does God's creative power expressed in verses 4–9 give you confidence that He can open new doors of purpose in your life?

How are God's compass and promise expressed in verses 10–11, and how do they direct you as you travel through loss?

PRAY that God would fill you with hope in Him, that He would give you patience and stillness to wait for Him to act, and that He would keep you from trying to find refuge in your own strength and solutions.

Future
WHEN PEACE INVADES UNEXPECTEDLY

Then [King Darius] was exceedingly glad, and commanded
that Daniel be taken up out of the den. So Daniel was
taken up out of the den, and no kind of harm was found
on him, because he had trusted in his God. (Daniel 6:23)

JOY

Are you ever surprised that, at times, in the middle of your
sadness and loss, you are doing really, really well? For some reason,
you experience moments of happiness. You laugh. You even feel . . .
normal. When you are with others, you have a sense that you're okay.
You can keep going and have strength to meet the day. This unexpected wellness defies what you anticipated in your grief. You thought
you would be falling apart all the time. You didn't realize you had any
wherewithal to face one of the most difficult challenges of your life,
but you're doing much better than you thought.

When sadness sweeps in and loss pounds you, the logical out-
come you envision for your life may be complete personal collapse.
You expect a dark valley, total despair, and absolute paralysis. But
suddenly and surprisingly, you may find yourself starting another
day with excitement, eating a meal with pleasure, enjoying a sunrise
with wonder, and talking to a friend with attentive interest. How
is it possible to explain this invasion of peace that provides normal,
fulfilling, and joyful moments?

A MIRACLE

Let's call it what it really is: a miracle. A miracle, after all, is an
astonishing occurrence that cannot be explained by science or logic.
Who could explain having any moments of tranquility or content-
ment after you have experienced one of the worst possible losses in
your life? When peace invades unexpectedly, it is not because of personal toughness, smarts, or strength. It is the work of God.

This truth is encouraging. If you're looking for God's presence in your pain, stay on the lookout for moments of peace, because Jesus provides peace that the world isn't able to give. God's Word assures every grieving heart of His presence: "The LORD is near to the brokenhearted and saves the crushed in spirit" (Psalm 34:18). This is what God does. From the deepest darkness, He creates the brightest light. He clears the most tangled pathways of sadness with His sustaining kindness and grace.

Consider the cry of Jesus from the darkness of the cross. As He carried the unimaginable weight of pain, brokenness, and sin, Jesus spoke words of forgiveness: "Father, forgive them, for they know not what they do" (Luke 23:34). He uttered a merciful statement of salvation: "Truly, I say to you, today you will be with Me in paradise" (Luke 23:43). He spoke of the certainty of our rescue and redemption: "It is finished" (John 19:30). Unexpected beauty burst from the ugliness of the cross.

Jesus pointed to the miraculous and gracious invasion of God's peace when He said, "Peace I leave with you; My peace I give to you. Not as the world gives do I give to you. Let not your hearts be troubled, neither let them be afraid" (John 14:27). Jesus gives what the world cannot. He provides peace that exceeds our strength and transcends our understanding. The apostle Paul urged his friends to rely on this gift that boggles the imagination and boosts morale: "Do not be anxious about anything, but in everything by prayer and supplication with thanksgiving let your requests be made known to God. And the peace of God, which surpasses all understanding, will guard your hearts and your minds in Christ Jesus" (Philippians 4:6–7).

The peace of God surpasses all understanding. Your unexplainable peace is evidence of God's presence. It is the gift of God's favor and the imprint of His miraculous grace in your life.

CELEBRATING PEACE

God has injected uncharacteristic joy into some very strange situations. After King Darius was coerced to throw his dear friend Daniel into the den of lions, the king exhibited classic symptoms of grief: he couldn't eat, he didn't want to do anything fun, and he couldn't sleep. All he could think about was the deception of his so-called advisers who tricked him into sentencing Daniel to certain death. Darius's heart broke. His soul grieved. He didn't know what to do. At daybreak the following morning, Darius ran to the den of lions. He cried out in despair, certain that all hope was lost and all joy had disappeared: "O Daniel, servant of the living God, has your God, whom you serve continually, been able to deliver you from the lions?" (Daniel 6:20). The king didn't expect to hear a reply. No one survived this ancient method of execution. It was impossible to expect any happiness in this grave situation. But out of the silence came Daniel's voice: "O king, live forever! My God sent His angel and shut the lions' mouths, and they have not harmed me" (Daniel 6:21–22).

A miracle of peace and joy overwhelmed heartbreak and loss. No other explanation would suffice. This was a resurrection. A stone was rolled over the opening of the lions' den with certain death in the cards. In the morning, the stone was rolled away, and life sprang forth. Daniel's miracle points to Jesus' resurrection and to our new life in Christ. This is the way God works. He sprinkles unexpected blessing into the mix of your sadness and pain.

King Darius, the leader of the Medo-Persian Empire with no roots in or connections to faith in the God of heaven, was led to write: "I make a decree, that in all my royal dominion people are to tremble and fear before the God of Daniel, for He is the living God, enduring forever; His kingdom shall never be destroyed, and His dominion shall be to the end. He delivers and rescues; He works signs and wonders in heaven and on earth, He who has saved Daniel from the power of the lions" (Daniel 6:26–27). You can almost hear the giddiness of joy and the unexpected peace in Darius's proclamation to the world.

The next time peace invades your heartbreak in an unexpected and surprising way, pause for a moment to recognize the goodness and presence of God. He is close. He saves. He pours unexplainable peace into your life. It's not only something that may make you smile, but it is also something you can tell the world.

WORDS FOR HEALING
Devotion Guide for Chapter Forty-Two

READ Psalm 41:1–3

REFLECT

These verses reference the weak and troubled. What do they tell you about God's attitude toward you when you are distressed?

When a psalm mentions enemies and foes, you may be able to equate your heartbreak to an adversary that is trying to overcome you. What peace does God provide even as you face difficulties?

How have you experienced God's encouraging peace and joy during your grief?

PRAY a prayer of thanksgiving to God for the times of joy and peace you've experienced unexpectedly. Thank Him for the miracle of His presence, help, and new life.

Fears

WHEN YOU'RE AFRAID

Then Boaz said to Ruth, "Now, listen, my daughter, do not go to glean in another field or leave this one, but keep close to my young women. Let your eyes be on the field that they are reaping, and go after them. Have I not charged the young men not to touch you? And when you are thirsty, go to the vessels and drink what the young men have drawn." (Ruth 2:8–9)

FEAR

What are you afraid of as you weather your grief? Do you wonder if you'll be all alone? Are you frightened that the emptiness you feel will never subside? Are you apprehensive about what you'll do next or where you'll go? Do you worry that people will abandon you or that you won't fit in anymore? Are you afraid that you won't be able to handle your life?

So much can strike fear in your heart when heartbreak strikes. Where does fear come from? Sometimes, panic arises from a belief that no one is looking out for you. Fear may sweep over you because you feel like your life is completely out of control. The prospect of facing life alone can cause you to dread the days ahead. The fear of feeling severe hurt and loss can create overwhelming anxiety in your heart.

Someone once told me that F-E-A-R stands for "Future Expectations Already Realized." When you're in a difficult place, it's hard not to look ahead and see only disaster looming. Thinking about the "what ifs" and playing out the worst-case scenarios come easily when the worst seems to have already happened. So much hurt has invaded. How can you not be terrified that the future holds even more pain? Fear is a by-product of one wound after another. You wait for the next shoe to drop, the next domino to fall, the next thing to go wrong. The dread of loss upon loss scares you.

DON'T BE AFRAID

That may be why one of the most common statements from God in the Bible is "Don't be afraid." When people faced difficult futures, God reached out to calm their fear. When challenging news had to be shared, God reassured His people to "fear not." When surprises shook people up, God was close to let them know there was no need to be frightened. When the prospects of hope looked dim, God's messengers reassured, "Do not be dismayed."

Fear is overcome only when a frightening future is filled with God's presence. That is why God revealed Himself in the past and why He makes Himself known to you today. Your Savior steps into the sadness and emptiness that make you tremble so you can be confident in His closeness and care. Throughout history, God fought fear by being present. He always showed up. Ultimately, He showed up in Jesus, who faced the most fearsome enemy when He died on the cross. But the resurrection of the Son of God gives you the assurance that although loss happens in your life, it is no longer the rule; it has become the exception. New life looms large when the risen Savior walks with you. No matter what this broken world brings, you do not have to be afraid.

SAFE PEOPLE AND PLACES

You may say, "That's easier said than done." But the beauty of God's fear-defeating work is that He doesn't just tell you not to be afraid; He does something about it. He provides a powerful and living Word to calm your heart and soul. He blesses you with His presence in the Lord's Supper so you do not have to rely on your strength alone. He gives you safe places and safe people to surround you with a sense of peace.

A woman named Ruth discovered that when she faced a frightening time. After her husband died, she left her homeland to travel with her mother-in-law, Naomi. Completely uprooted, thoroughly broken emotionally, and facing an uncertain future in a place she had never been, Ruth spoke some of the most well-known words in the Bible. She said to Naomi, "Where you go I will go, and where you lodge I will lodge. Your people shall be my people, and your God my God. Where you die I will die, and there will I be buried. May the LORD do so to me and more also if anything but death parts me from you" (Ruth 1:16–17). She expressed total commitment. But then, life became even more frightening.

The two women traveled to Bethlehem, Naomi's hometown. Having nothing and desperately needing food, young Ruth ventured out to the field to pick up crops left over from the harvest. A man named Boaz saw her and befriended her. He said to her, "Now, listen, my daughter, do not go to glean in another field or leave this one, but keep close to my young women. Let your eyes be on the field that they are reaping, and go after them. Have I not charged the young men not to touch you? And when you are thirsty, go to the vessels and drink what the young men have drawn."

Boaz was a safe person who provided a safe place for Ruth. She didn't have to be afraid. As the days unfolded for Ruth and Naomi, Boaz became an advocate for these dear women in need. Eventually, he became Ruth's husband. Ruth and Boaz had a son, the delight of grandmother Naomi's heart and a boy who would grow up to be King David's grandfather. God showed up to replace fear with heart-mending blessing.

Here is a truth for your life: there may be many reasons to fear, but they are no match for the reality of God's faithfulness. As God cared about Ruth, He cares deeply about you too. Today, He whispers, "Don't be afraid."

As you face your future, look for the safe people God provides. A trusted friend, a loving parent, a helpful mentor, a caring pastor—God does not forget you or abandon you. He creates community to help calm your fears. Look for the safe places your Savior gives: your church, a friend's family room, a group of people who refill your hope and help restore your soul. In your journey through heartbreak and loss, look for God's dependable action and steadfast love. He is present to calm your fear.

WORDS FOR HEALING
Devotion Guide for Chapter Forty-Three

READ Psalm 56

REFLECT

Many of the psalms speak openly about facing enemies. Sometimes, the enemy in your life is cruel loss that leads to fear. How do verses 1–4 provide you with fortification to face your fears?

The writer of this psalm expresses an agonizing struggle as he recounts his hurt and tears. How can you relate to what he says in verses 5–11?

A refrain is repeated in verse 4 and in verses 10–11. How might this refrain become yours as you deal with what makes you afraid?

PRAY verses 12–13, letting God know your reasons for giving Him thanks and telling Him how you would like to serve Him as an expression of your gratitude. Thank Him for keeping your feet from falling and for specific ways you now walk in the light of life.

Fears

WHEN YOU DON'T THINK YOU'LL MAKE IT OUT OF THIS ALIVE

Then [Jesus] said to them, "My soul is very sorrowful, even to death; remain here, and watch with Me." (Matthew 26:38)

ANGUISH

If you feel like letting go because of your hurt and heartbreak, don't let go just yet. Jesus meets you in the darkest and most distant corners of your life. He's been where you are, and He will lead you through. You may not feel an ounce of strength, but Jesus' power can bring you through your weakness. You may have no sense of optimism, but Jesus holds hope for you and will carry you out of your anguish. You don't need to understand anything or try to get control of anything when grief causes your system to crash. Just breathe, be still, and let your Savior sustain you.

You've probably heard about people who have died from a broken heart. You may feel that way right now—so overwhelmed that you can't go on, so overcome with sorrow that your heart can barely keep beating. You are in darkness so thick and oppressive that you can barely gasp for breath. Your sadness and tears may even be leading you to despair of your own life. You're tired and feel that it needs to be over. But Jesus speaks to you in your anguish—not as an outsider or bystander, but as a fellow sufferer who truly understands the weight and enormity of your pain. As Jesus spoke to His disciples in the Garden of Gethsemane, He speaks to you today: "My soul is very sorrowful, even to death; remain here, and watch with Me."

Did you hear how Jesus feels what you feel and understands what you suffer? He knows the crushing agony of a broken heart. He experienced sorrow that made Him feel as if His life was ending. The strain of utter sadness and despair drove Jesus to the point of not wanting to endure the agony any longer. But His words also bring help. In the depths of His own darkness, Jesus spoke words that grab hold of you and steady you in your darkness: "Remain here, and watch with Me."

Don't go anywhere in your anguish. Don't run off alone in your pain. Remain with Jesus. Stay with Him. Abide in Him. Throw all of your hopelessness and despair upon His shoulders. Tell Him it is His responsibility because you can't handle it any longer. Make no decisions in your weariness. Take no action when you're tired. Just remain where you are and watch with Jesus. Look for the way He will step up and do what He is supposed to do. Wait for Him to make the first move. If you feel like descending deeper into your hopelessness, if you feel like you won't make it out of this loss alive, collapse before Jesus. Then heed His words: wait, stop, remain with Him, and watch.

YOUR COMPANION IN GRIEF

Despair is never meant to be endured alone. That's why Jesus brought His disciples with Him to Gethsemane. And that is why God draws close to you during your darkest hours. He speaks to your aching heart: "Fear not, for I have redeemed you; I have called you by name, you are Mine. When you pass through the waters, I will be with you; and through the rivers, they shall not overwhelm you; when you walk through fire you shall not be burned, and the flame shall not consume you. For I am the LORD your God, the Holy One of Israel, your Savior" (Isaiah 43:1–3).

Your life is of utter importance to God. He doesn't keep His distance when you struggle with the agony of loss and sadness. He draws even closer to you. He speaks your name and calls you His own. He feels the crashing waves of pain with you. He endures the suffocating waters of grief just as you do. He struggles with the flames of adversity as a friend walking by your side. And He will bring you through it all. It may not seem possible. The present moments of pain may seem too strong. Your desire to survive may have drained away long ago. But Jesus needs you and cares about you. He does not want you to suffer alone. That is why He promised, "I am with you always, to the end of the age" (Matthew 28:20). Remain with Him. Watch what He will do. See how He will carry you through the darkness.

YOUR BEST COURSE OF ACTION

Is it possible to put a stop to your suffering? It is so exhausting to be sad. Heartbreak is absolutely draining. Is there any immediate solution? As you walk through the agonizing pain of loss, it is important to remember that your perspective is skewed. Your perception and thought processes do not have complete clarity when you are grieving. Your reactions and solutions are coming from places that are depleted and spent. Heartbreak is never a time to make big decisions or to take significant action.

Notice what Jesus did when He was sorrowful to the point of death: He stayed with people, He went to a garden, He prayed, and He sought God's will. Jesus couldn't "solve" His grief, but He did approach it with life-replenishing practices. He walked this pathway under the greatest pressure possible in order to lead you through your oppressive sadness.

Jesus stayed with people. Like Jesus, you need the perspective and presence of people who are not overwhelmed with suffering. Be careful about isolating yourself. Talk to a friend or counselor. Don't go it alone.

Jesus went to a garden. Bringing trusted friends with Him, Jesus went to a life-giving context. The Garden of Gethsemane offered a place of refuge in the middle of bustling Jerusalem. In your heartbreak, find the sanctuary spaces that refill your soul. Be in places that promote life and peace.

While in the garden, Jesus prayed. Prayer was His lifeline. You, too, have been given that precious gift. Pour out your heart to your heavenly Father, who loves you, listens to you, and carries your burdens. Keep talking to Him.

In prayer, Jesus sought His Father's leadership and guidance. Jesus cried out, "My Father, if it be possible, let this cup pass from Me, nevertheless, not as I will, but as You will" (Matthew 26:39). Searching the Scriptures allows you to receive the sustaining, replenishing, and guiding will of God. Seek God's help in His Word of life.

If you are bottoming out in despair and are ready for your life to end, don't do anything except remain with Jesus. Watch for Him to take full responsibility for you. His grace-filled action of restoration, help, and relief will come through.

WORDS FOR HEALING

Devotion Guide for Chapter Forty-Four

READ Psalm 94:17–19

REFLECT

How can you relate to the total dependence on God expressed in verses 17–19?

How have you seen God's love supporting you during your heartbreak?

Verse 19 brings the good news that God brings consolation when your cares and anxiety are overwhelming. What consolation from God have you seen lately?

PRAY that God will sustain you with His steadfast love and give you the help you need so desperately during your overwhelming despair. Ask Him to stay close to you and not let you go.

Fears

WHEN YOU'RE AFRAID TO FEEL AGAIN

But [Thomas] said to [the disciples], "Unless I see
in His hands the mark of the nails, and place my
finger into the mark of the nails, and place my hand
into His side, I will never believe." (John 20:25)

SHUT DOWN?

Who would ever want to venture again into the possibility of
heartbreak? It is much too overwhelming to feel loss. Why take the
risk of getting your hopes up just to experience a crushing letdown?
When you think about venturing into the territory of trusting and
feeling again, you may resist any prospect that could bring hurt. You
may never want to go there again.

But is this where you'll be for the rest of your life? Should you
shut down your feelings for good? Is it now your lot in life to lead
a guarded and emotionless existence? In order to avoid the lows of
loss, should you shut down the risks, relationships, and opportunities that may fulfill your heart's desires?

It's tempting to try to live that way, but it's not possible. You may
be successful in avoiding new loss, but when the walls go up, the old
loss makes a thriving home in your heart. In order to let your current grief move on, you need to open your heart to the frightening
possibility that grief will come again. But you're not alone in that
terrifying territory.

RESTORED

A man named Thomas was afraid to feel again. As one of Jesus'
disciples, Thomas has the reputation for being a doubter, a skeptic,
the hesitant follower who always looked before he leaped. He has
been labeled "doubting Thomas." If people hesitate to buy in or to
believe, they become a doubting Thomas too.

But Thomas wasn't always tentative and resistant. Before his
episode of doubt in John 20, Thomas was bold and daring. He was

the courageous apostle who wore his heart on his sleeve and threw himself fully into his relationship with Jesus. When Jesus decided to go back to the area where His enemies wanted to kill Him, Thomas spoke up passionately and said to his fellow disciples, "Let us also go, that we may die with Him" (John 11:16). After Jesus announced that He would go and prepare a place for His disciples, Thomas piped up, "Lord, we do not know where You are going. How can we know the way?" (John 14:5).

Thomas was the guy who blurted out the question everyone was thinking. He invested all of his hopes, all of his love, and all of his devotion in Jesus.

That's why it hurt so much when Jesus was crucified. In your struggle with loss, you may be able to imagine the devastating loss Thomas felt when he saw his Teacher, his Leader, his Friend, and his Savior beaten, abused, and killed on a cross. The grief may have impacted him so strongly that he couldn't bear to be with the other disciples when Jesus appeared to them the first time in John 20. The disciples were together in a locked room, but Thomas wasn't there. He was on the run. So the disciples reached out to Thomas and told him the remarkable news that they had seen Jesus. But Thomas answered, "Unless I see in His hands the mark of the nails, and place my finger into the mark of the nails, and place my hand into His side, I will never believe."

Those are not just words of stubborn resistance or cynical doubt. They are words filled with the woundedness that comes from profound loss. You may know exactly where Thomas was coming from. How could he again go to that place of trust, love, and hope? How could he risk the hurt that broke his heart so deeply? How could he venture out and live normally again when his feelings were still so tender and his emotions were still so fragile? So, he resisted. "Never," he said. "I will never believe unless I am totally certain."

When you are afraid to open the door to your feelings, Jesus will serve as the faithful doorkeeper who opens the way to hope, trust, and love again. Your Savior will do for you what He did for Thomas. First, Jesus provided some faithful friends. The disciples reached out to Thomas and brought him back to the group. In your pain, people will be reaching out to you. You may not hear them right away, and you may need some space for a while, but there is a time to let them embrace you, console you, and be with you. As He did for Thomas,

Jesus will send people your way. Then, eight days after His first appearance, Jesus came to His disciples again—Thomas included. At just the right time, Jesus approached and appeared. When you are hurting with grief and loss, you don't have to jump into the risk of being hurt again. In His time, Jesus will faithfully and gently guide you where you need to go. There is no hurry or pressure. Let your Savior console your heart and give you the faith and courage you need. Jesus, who is risen and alive, will walk with you to show you the way.

Then Jesus spoke to Thomas. Notice that Jesus didn't scold the fragile and shaken disciple. The risen Savior didn't speak harsh words of disappointment. Jesus said, "Peace be with you." Then He reassured Thomas by inviting him, "Put your finger here, and see My hands; and put out your hand, and place it in My side. Do not disbelieve, but believe" (John 20:26–27). It was safe to believe again. It was okay to hope and reengage. Death did not win. Fear would not prevail. Loss could never have the last word.

When you are afraid to feel again, Jesus will restore your heart, renew your hope, and rekindle your love in His time. He will equip you to reenter your emotional life without fear. He will draw close to you and deal gently with your fragile feelings and your tender heart.

After Jesus spoke to Thomas, the strengthened disciple replied, "My Lord and my God!" (John 20:28). He was back—back to a place where he could boldly believe again, back to a place where he felt safe in expressing his love and devotion. If you're afraid right now, take heart. Jesus will bring you back.

WORDS FOR HEALING

Devotion Guide for Chapter Forty-Five

READ Psalm 115:9–18

REFLECT

Verses 9–11 repeat the calling to trust in the Lord because He is our help and shield. How does this repeated encouragement help you when you are afraid?

Verses 12–13 speak wonderful promises that God will remember you and bless you. How do these assurances give you strength as you look to your future?

The final verses of this psalm make it clear that we are God's living people who give Him praise. What does this truth tell you about God's gracious work for your heart when it feels lifeless because of pain and loss?

PRAY that God will put life and faith into your heart again, that He will remove fear that immobilizes you, and that He will graciously restore you at the right time so you can live a life of hope, trust, and love.

Fears

WHEN YOU'RE OVERCOME BY ANXIETY

And being in agony [Jesus] prayed more earnestly;
and His sweat became like great drops of blood
falling down to the ground. (Luke 22:44)

ANXIETY

Your heartbreak will always show itself in some way. The effects of loss will become apparent, even when you do the best you can to live normally or as you try to muster up courage in the face of anxiety and pain. As grief simmers below the surface of your life, you may be overcome by anxiety. Heart palpitations may show your stress and strain. You may experience moments of panic—or full-on panic attacks. Tears may flow suddenly and for unpredictable reasons. Fear may paralyze you at unexpected moments. You may struggle through sleepless nights.

In your grief, your intellectual desire to avoid heartbreak's pain cannot overcome your physical and emotional reaction to it. No matter how strong and determined you are, your loss will manifest itself in some way. Because you have lost an important and precious part of your life, you will experience the emptiness, sadness, and weakness grief brings. But when your weakness makes itself known, God's strength is ready to step in as the steady and helpful remedy. God said to the apostle Paul in his anxiety and pain, "My grace is sufficient for you, for My power is made perfect in weakness" (2 Corinthians 12:9). When you experience loss, you will need rest, you will need consolation, you may need counseling from a professional, and you may need medication to help you through the physical and emotional impact of anxiety. But in addition to those practical and therapeutic answers to your grief, you will need strength and solutions beyond what this world can provide. Grief strikes so deeply in the heart that only divine solutions can provide enduring help.

WEAKNESS AND STRENGTH

The simple but profound song "Jesus Loves Me" wisely states, "Little ones to Him belong; they are weak, but He is strong." You may not want to admit your weaknesses, but if you've been around for any time at all, you know that your limitations, vulnerabilities, and weaknesses show up on a regular basis. And when grief barges in, you are brought to a new level of need. The anxiety of loss can crush you under its oppressive load. That is why, in your weakness, God pursues you with His strength.

The resurrection of Jesus from the dead overcame the anxiety-inducing effect of death, loss, and heartbreak. The apostle Paul declared, " 'O death, where is your victory? O death, where is your sting?' The sting of death is sin, and the power of sin is the law. But thanks be to God, who gives us the victory through our Lord Jesus Christ" (1 Corinthians 15:55–57). Jesus defeated the power of anxiety by wrestling with it to His death and rising from it to new life. You may be weak. Your anxiety may be overwhelming. But Jesus is strong. He is with you to carry your worries, fears, and terror.

You may remember the time when Jesus prayed in the Garden of Gethsemane the night before His death. Luke's Gospel reports that "His sweat became like great drops of blood falling down to the ground." Luke was a doctor. He noticed the physical symptoms of stress. Some believe that blood became mingled with Jesus' sweat as capillaries burst in His forehead due to the overwhelming stress of facing death for the sin of the world. Clearly, Jesus stepped into extreme anxiety that is impossible to comprehend. But because of His suffering, Jesus can understand the anxiety you suffer. And because He made His way through the most severe anguish possible, Jesus can bring you through the suffocating torment you feel.

A promise in Romans 6 provides hope when anxiety grips you: "We were buried therefore with [Jesus] by baptism into death, in order that, just as Christ was raised from the dead by the glory of the Father, we too might walk in newness of life" (v. 4). You are weak, but Jesus is strong. Yes, Jesus loves you too much to leave you alone in your anxiety. He will walk with you in newness of life; He will console you and strengthen you.

WATCHFUL AND PRAYERFUL

But as you may know, anxiety keeps stalking you when you suffer loss. You can feel the worries well up in your throat. The rigors of your own hurt combine with the tone of an anxious world to ramp up your stress and apprehension. The fast pace of life doesn't help. Your busy schedule sends you running frantically. The overwhelming supply of bad news creates a baseline of fear that intensifies the anxiety you feel. It can seem like a losing battle.

But when anxiety hits with full force, Jesus brings an answer. Even as anxiety prowls, your strong Savior provides the pathway to peace. Jesus said to His disciples as they were gathered together in the Garden of Gethsemane, "Watch and pray that you may not enter into temptation" (Matthew 26:41). Jesus invited His followers to be alert and watchful as exhaustion from sorrow tried to take hold. What were they supposed to watch for? The work of God. What did the disciples see? They witnessed a teacher who continued to guide them through this stressful time. They saw a Savior who loved them so much that He was willing to sacrifice His life for them. And they even saw an angel from heaven appear in the garden to strengthen Jesus as He suffered agonizing distress (Luke 22:43).

When you are suffering because of anxious times, be watchful for God's miraculous and caring help. In His faithfulness, He will show up when you need Him most.

Jesus also bid His disciples to pray. The power of prayer is not as much in your speaking as it is in God's listening. Implicit in prayer is the promise that God hears you and responds. When you are overcome by anxiety, you can cast your cares upon your Lord and Savior, being confident that He will carry the burden and lighten your load.

Watch and pray. You have a Savior who loves you and brings consolation to your overwhelmed and overstressed soul.

WORDS FOR HEALING
Devotion Guide for Chapter Forty-Six

READ Psalm 28:6–9

REFLECT

What comfort is it that God promises to hear your cries for help during times of distress (v. 6)?

Verse 7 emphasizes how our hearts are helped by God. How does this verse reflect the help you have received and still hope to receive from God?

How do verses 8–9 emphasize your ongoing dependence on God's strength and help?

PRAY for God's peace during your anxiety. As you watch and pray, ask God to open your eyes to see the help He provides. Ask Him to listen to your cries and to respond with mercy.

Fears

WHEN IT HURTS MORE THAN IT EVER HAS

Then one of the twelve, whose name was Judas Iscariot, went to the chief priests and said, "What will you give me if I deliver Him over to you?" And they paid him thirty pieces of silver. And from that moment he sought an opportunity to betray Him. (Matthew 26:14–16)

ESCAPE

Hurting more than you ever have is frightening. During this deep and abiding pain, you may be tempted to try to escape from it. You may want to numb the ache in your soul and find respite from your serious wounds of grief and loss. Flight is a normal reaction to anguish. No one wants to hurt. But the desire to escape can lead to dangerous territory.

Self-destructive and addictive behaviors may seem desirable during seasons of heartbreak. You may feel the urge to lose yourself in drugs or alcohol. But the cycle of chemical anesthetizing will only send you spiraling deeper into pain with a more depleted and de-pendent emotional state. You may be lured into spending money in excess in order to experience the temporary buzz of material comfort. But the things you buy can never fill the empty spaces in your heart. Your yearning for wholeness may catapult you into sexual careless-ness. But rebounding from grief into reckless relationships will only add guilt and confusion to your already overwhelmed heart. In your depleted emotional condition, you may seek the rush of adrenaline brought by unwise risks. But while putting yourself in danger buys you a few moments to forget your pain, it imposes ongoing stress and worry on the ones you love.

Escape is a poor substitute for rest. When loss and pain invade your life, it is tempting to bypass healthy restoration and leap into destructive avoidance. Escape presents itself as a fast and fairly easy solution, but in reality it is a complicated and constraining web that multiplies pain and holds you captive to loss. The temporary numbness that escape offers as you hurt deceives you into believing you're okay. But escape stuffs grief deeper into your soul, never allowing you to take healthy steps through it. Instead, escape builds a reservoir of loss that will continue to overwhelm you.

Judas, the disciple who betrayed Jesus, is a case study in trying to escape pain. You may know his tragic story. When Jesus made it clear that He was not on earth to rebel against the Roman Empire or to establish a temporal kingdom, Judas decided to force Jesus' hand. He orchestrated a confrontation between Jesus and the religious leaders seeking His life. With a kiss, Judas singled out his Rabbi in the Garden of Gethsemane. But instead of leading a rebellion, Jesus went peacefully to His eventual brutal suffering and death. The Gospel writer Matthew reported the result of Judas's action: "When Judas, His betrayer, saw that Jesus was condemned, he changed his mind and brought back the thirty pieces of silver to the chief priests and the elders, saying, 'I have sinned by betraying innocent blood.' They said, 'What is that to us? See to it yourself.' And throwing down the pieces of silver into the temple, he departed, and he went and hanged himself" (Matthew 27:3–5).

This is a very difficult episode in the Bible. It brings the brutal reality of pain and loss to the surface. It exposes the raw emotions and dark dangers of deep heartbreak. But it also shows the destructive results of grasping for escape from pain instead of seeking rest. Jesus wants you to receive rest. He doesn't want you to be lost in denial or escape. He said, "Come to Me, all who labor and are heavy laden, and I will give you rest. Take My yoke upon you, and learn from Me, for I am gentle and lowly in heart, and you will find rest for your souls. For My yoke is easy, and My burden is light" (Matthew 11:28–30).

REST

That is the ongoing invitation of Jesus. During an overwhelming season in the disciples' lives, Jesus showed that rest was the answer. When their activity level was overwhelming and they couldn't even take a break to eat, Jesus said to His disciples, "Come away by yourselves to a desolate place and rest a while" (Mark 6:31). Jesus called His followers to stop and to experience a time of refreshment and restoration. Their getaway wasn't avoidance or denial; it was a healthy pause in the action in order to be restored in the presence of Jesus. The disciples were being called to face the fact of their fatigue and to take time out to deal with it.

God doesn't want you to avoid your hurt; He wants to heal your hurt. Judas took escape to its tragic extreme, but Peter walked the pathway of rest. You may recall that Peter also denied Jesus. He also ran away from his Savior and left Him in the hands of those who would kill Him. He wept bitterly and felt the sting of remorse and regret. But instead of seeking the numbing destruction of escape, Peter went fishing. He stepped into the quiet rhythm of what replenished his soul. And that is where Jesus met him. After His resurrection, Jesus sought Peter at the seashore. Jesus invited Peter to eat breakfast. Then, in a quiet yet challenging conversation, Jesus restored Peter and gave him a new beginning. Jesus said to the humbled disciple, "Feed My sheep. . . . Follow Me" (John 21:18–19).

When loss enters your life, it is of utmost importance to receive regular rest. A healthy rhythm of replenishment is a crucial antidote to the strain of heartbreak. This isn't complicated. You can seek refuge in the simple pattern of a balanced life. There is a time for work and a time for relaxation. There is a time to be connected and a time to unplug. For equilibrium in your life, you need the essential elements of a healthy diet, physical exercise, regular sleep, ongoing prayer, quiet reflection, and building relationships with others. You weather the pain of grief through counseling, conversation, community, time in God's Word, time in worship, and time for recovery. A rhythm of rest in the company of Jesus can carry you through the rigors of grief's restlessness. There is no need to escape. There is no need to run anywhere except into your Savior's arms. He will make you whole again.

WORDS FOR HEALING

Devotion Guide for Chapter Forty-Seven

READ Psalm 32:1–7

REFLECT

How do verses 1–5 capture the contrast of trying to escape or deny heartbreak versus seeking rest in God's help?

What temptations to escape are you facing in your hurt, and how is God directing you to find rest in Him?

What hope and promises do you find in verses 6–7 that steer you away from avoidance and point you to seeking refuge in your Savior?

PRAY that God would protect you from unhealthy efforts to numb your pain. Ask Him to lead you to His restoration, to open your heart to His Word of life, and to become your dependable hiding place as you walk through grief.

Love

WHEN YOU MISS THE ONE YOU LOVE

Martha said to Jesus, "Lord, if You had been
here, my brother would not have died. But
even now I know that whatever You ask from
God, God will give You." (John 11:21–22)

A PRECIOUS PERSON

Grief is often connected intimately to people you care about in
a profound way. Sadness strikes deep in your heart when someone
you love is taken from you. You miss that person. You yearn for their
smile and laughter, their smell and embrace, their conversation and
personality. You crave their tangible and real-life presence. You want
to see them and be with them. The void left by losing someone you
love can be absolutely unbearable. How terrible it is to be alone, to
be without the person you cherished and poured your life into. You
don't want that person to be gone. You dread the possibility of forgetting the daily details that you may have taken for granted at one
time. But when that precious person is gone, you miss him; you hurt
for her presence.

What can ever help you cope with the pain of losing someone you
love? I don't think you ever "get over" losing a loved one. I am convinced that you are gradually forced to become accustomed to their
absence. That's right, I said forced.

Think about it: no one chooses heartbreak. Grief is thrust into
your life by a broken and chaotic existence in this fallen world. We
lose people. We are tragically and hurtfully separated from people
we would never choose to leave. When they are gone, do you have a
choice to do anything but adjust?

Of course, you can fight that adjustment. You can become a
bitter, resistant, and despairing person. You can rage against God,
others, and yourself as you face your terrible anguish and unwanted
adversity. But you're still making an adjustment. It's a poor one, but

you're changing into a sour human being because of your sadness. There is, however, another way. To the coerced and unpleasant reality of your heartbreak, Jesus brings the only hope possible: restoration.

RESTORATION

Psalm 23 says about God, your Good Shepherd, "He restores my soul" (v. 3). The fact that God is involved in soul restoration highlights the reality of soul wreckage. When someone you love is lost from your life, your soul becomes hurt, battered, confused, empty, and angry. Your soul becomes wrecked. It is like a once-fine home that has lost its loving inhabitants and has become a run-down fixer-upper. You may not even want anyone to occupy your soul again. Your desire may be to keep your soul on the overgrown back lot of your life—never going there again, never wanting to take the chance on filling it with loving inhabitants. But Jesus knows that a vacant soul is not a safe place. It has no joy and embraces no hope. It is sad and lonely and lost. For such soul wreckage, Jesus steps forward with restoration.

How does this work? What does Jesus do to restore a soul that feels beyond restoration? It may help to see Jesus in action. In John 11, Mary and Martha experienced the crushing loss of their brother, Lazarus. Friends and family gathered to console the saddened sisters. Then Martha heard that Jesus was on His way. She left the house and went out to meet Him. Her first reaction was to tell Jesus that this wreckage should have never happened. She said, "Lord, if You had been here, my brother would not have died. But even now I know that whatever You ask from God, God will give You."

But Jesus turned the conversation in a different direction. Seeing His precious friend wounded from grief and fearful of life without her brother, Jesus spoke words of hope that removed the finality from Martha's hurt and loss. He said to her, "Your brother will rise again." Martha moved from regret and wreckage to faith and hope. She responded, "I know that he will rise again in the resurrection on the last day." Then Jesus gave her the only possible help that exists when you miss someone you love. He said, "I am the resurrection and the life. Whoever believes in Me, though he die, yet shall he live, and everyone who lives and believes in Me shall never die" (John 11:23–26).

What restores a wounded and wrecked soul? The remarkable and refreshing truth that loss does not have the last word. By faith in Jesus, the promise of the resurrection and an eternal reunion brings renewal to wrecked and hurting souls. Walking in faith with ones you love will keep you together in Christ forever. Missing a loved one will cause serious hurt, but because of Jesus, the pain will not last forever.

But what if your loved one did not walk in faith? What if he or she did not know and believe in Jesus? What can help a wounded soul then? The same faith in Jesus who is the resurrection and the life. Even if you are completely uncertain about your loved one's trust in Jesus, you can still seek refuge in the Savior who brings you restoration and help. You can still place all your hope in Him. I'm not asking you to pretend a loved one had faith or to grasp onto false hope. I'm simply saying that your Savior still holds you in His hands and will faithfully minister to your soul no matter what happens. He will make sure you are okay. He will heal you. He will take the wrecked old house you're in and make it a mansion beyond your imagination—because He loves you and is trustworthy. He will remove your pain and make you whole again.

Jesus asked Martha an important question at the end of their conversation. He said to her, "Do you believe this?" With Lazarus still in the tomb, Martha's soul was brought back to life. She answered, "Yes, Lord; I believe that You are the Christ, the Son of God, who is coming into the world" (John 11:26–27).

Jesus asks you the same question today. As you miss your loved one, He asks whether you believe that He is your resurrection and life. He inquires if you believe that He can heal you and restore your soul. Today, Jesus gives you faith, strength, and encouragement to answer, "Yes, Lord; I believe."

WORDS FOR HEALING
Devotion Guide for Chapter Forty-Eight

READ Psalm 36:5–9

REFLECT

Sometimes you need to be reminded that God knows what He is doing and that He is completely faithful. How do verses 5–6 help restore your trust in Him?

Even as you face great loss, how do verses 7–9 restore your soul with the hope of life?

To whom in your life do you need to talk about faith in Jesus?

PRAY for God's restoration as you travel through sadness and pain. Ask Him to fill you with hope and trust in Him. Thank Him for overcoming death through Jesus' death and resurrection. Ask Him to help you share that life-giving news with loved ones in your life.

Love
WHEN YOU NEED A HUG

So Barnabas went to Tarsus to look for Saul. (Acts 11:25)

SIMPLE COMFORT

Grief can be extremely complicated. A tangle of intricate feelings and needs can course through your heart and mind. From moment to moment, your experience with loss can throw you quickly from one emotional place to another. At times, you may not understand what you're going through. But sometimes, your heartbreak is very simple. It's downright easy. You're not wrestling with difficult intellectual places or deep yearnings of the heart or demanding questions of the soul. You just need a hug. You need a trusted friend to come alongside and embrace you. You need to bury your face in someone's shoulder and sob for a while. You need a caring and compassionate person to encourage you and shed a tear with you. In your heartbreak, you don't always need complex help; sometimes, you just need to be held.

Isn't it puzzling how simple comfort can be forgotten when sadness strikes? Some people want you to express anger that may be brewing inside. Others urge you to be verbal so you can process all the feelings you're experiencing. There are those who tell you to get busy with a protective prescription of ideas and activities that will ward off gloom and despair. But too often, love is forgotten. Psychological understanding is important. Emotional therapy is a beneficial blessing. Counseling and programs and fixes may be helpful. But sometimes, you need what the apostle Paul called "the greatest" of all qualities—human and divine. You need that which never fails. You need love. You need a hug.

AN ENCOURAGING EMBRACE

It's no accident that "God is love" is one of the most profound definitions of God revealed in the Scriptures (1 John 4:16). Love is not a wimpy emotion for weaklings. Love is not an impulsive and flighty activity for feeling-driven lightweights. Love is bold and courageous. It is completely self-sacrificial. We understand what love truly is, the Bible tells us, by seeing how Jesus laid down His life for us as a sacrifice for our sins (1 John 3:16). Love is patient and kind. It protects, hopes, trusts, and perseveres. It never fails (1 Corinthians 13:4–8). Love drives out fear (1 John 4:18). Love is so powerful, it can stare death in the eyes and meet it blow for blow (Song of Solomon 8:6). The primary hallmark of a follower of Jesus is not spiritual insight or intellectual understanding or holiness of life, but an abiding love for Jesus and for one another (John 13:35).

Is it any mystery, therefore, why love is such an important and effective antidote for loss? Love is the greatest help for healing heartbreak.

This simple truth is seen so clearly in the life of a man named Barnabas. We're told that his name means "son of encouragement" (Acts 4:36). Barnabas stands out as the person who befriended Saul, the man who persecuted followers of Jesus but experienced a complete change and became a proclaimer of Christ. Everyone who confessed faith in Jesus was afraid of Saul. Was he faking his faith in order to infiltrate the Church? Would he turn on believers, betray their confidence, and throw them into prison? Saul was taboo. Even courageous Peter cowered in fear when he heard about Saul. That's when Barnabas came along and vouched for the former villain. The Book of Acts tells us, "Barnabas took [Saul] and brought him to the apostles and declared to them how on the road he had seen the Lord, who spoke to him, and how at Damascus he had preached boldly in the name of Jesus. So he went in and out among them at Jerusalem, preaching boldly in the name of the Lord" (Acts 9:27–28). Barnabas showed simple love and compassion. He didn't let the complexity of the situation interfere with what was needed most. Barnabas stepped in as the encourager who embraced Saul. And he did it more than once.

Because Saul turned on his fellow tormentors, they became determined to kill him. That's when Saul was sent back to the safety of his hometown, Tarsus. He waited there for nearly a decade. Can you imagine how Saul felt? At one time, he was on top of the world, the leader of Pharisees in the cause against Christianity. He was respected and admired by his peers as a learned and powerful man. But now, as a new follower of Jesus, he lost everything. The bad guys hated him, and the good guys were afraid of him. He sat at home wondering if he would be of any use to anyone.

But Barnabas remembered Saul. When a new movement of faith began to develop among residents in the city of Antioch, the apostles sent Barnabas there to encourage the new believers and to share the Gospel with more people. As momentum built, Barnabas did something amazing. Acts 11 says, "So Barnabas went to Tarsus to look for Saul, and when he had found him, he brought him to Antioch. For a whole year they met with the church and taught a great many people. And in Antioch the disciples were first called Christians" (Acts 11:25–26).

Once again, Barnabas cut through the static of loneliness, sadness, and loss with an encouraging embrace. He went to look for Saul. He traveled nearly 150 miles each way on the road from Antioch to Tarsus and back. He found the man in need, put his arm around him, and asked him to join him in a fulfilling and exciting task. You may know the rest of the story as Saul's name changed to Paul, and he became one of the most transformational influences for Jesus in the history of the world. It all started with simple love and encouragement.

All of us need a Barnabas or two. When you're down, you need someone to lift you up. Today, you can know that Jesus embraces you with His grace and encourages you with His steadfast love and forgiveness. Jesus is always a dependable Barnabas in your life. And He will send you people filled with His love to cut through grief's complications. He will provide you with caring people who can show you simple compassion in your sadness. Jesus loves you so much, and He knows you need to be held in your heartbreak and to be loved as you grieve loss. When the complexity of grief starts to swirl around you and within you, don't be afraid to find a trusted and caring person Jesus places in your life. Then ask for a hug.

WORDS FOR HEALING
Devotion Guide for Chapter Forty-Nine

READ Psalm 146

REFLECT

According to verses 1–4, God is worthy of praise because He can do what no person can accomplish. What gracious work of God do you need during your time of loss?

In what ways do verses 5–9 describe how God embraces His people?

How does verse 10 give you confidence when you feel unloved and alone?

PRAY that God would embrace you with the encouragement of His Word and the love of His people. Ask for a friend to seek you, hear you, understand you, and show you compassion when you need it most.

Love
WHEN YOU'VE LOST YOUR WHOLE WORLD

Simeon blessed them and said to Mary His mother, "Behold, this child is appointed for the fall and rising of many in Israel, and for a sign that is opposed (and a sword will pierce through your own soul also)." (Luke 2:34–35)

INVESTMENT

When you invest your life in someone or something important to you, the hurt of rejection and loss is multiplied. Pour your life into a child only to experience being pushed away, and you know what it feels like to lose your whole world. Work for decades at a job, giving the best you can, only to be impersonally dismissed, and you know the sting of a shattered world. Give of yourself in marriage year after year only to be abandoned by an uncaring spouse, and you know the pain of loss. Become vulnerable and sacrificial as you invest in a relationship only to be snubbed and cast aside, and you know the emptiness of a broken heart. Walk with a loved one for a lifetime only to lose them to heartbreaking death, and you are well acquainted with the sword of grief that can pierce your soul.

One of the biggest myths in any life pursuit is the phrase "Don't take it personally." But what isn't personal isn't important. When you take the risk to pour your heart into a relationship or an endeavor, it is very personal. And when loss strikes, it hurts. You're left feeling empty, slighted, and even betrayed. You wonder if any of your identity is still intact. When you invest love and time in what is truly important to you, the pain of loss is intensified. Is the risk worth it?

THE FOOTSTEPS OF GOD

I'm going to tell you it is. You can avoid grief by refusing to feel anything toward anyone. You can bypass hurt if you protect yourself with walls that seal off passion, joy, and devotion. You can keep heartbreak out of your life if you stay uninterested in anything and uninvolved with anyone. But that loss would be much greater than any heartbreak resulting from living a fully invested life. Taking the risk to love is taking the risk to be a person, to be human. Much more than that, taking the risk to love means to follow boldly in the footsteps of God.

God created human beings in His own image and likeness. They were set apart from all of creation not only because of their uniqueness as creatures but because of the love and devotion God showered upon them. God took the risk to invest His heart in humanity. But then God was betrayed. Human beings prioritized selfish ambition over their Creator and walked away from their intimate relationship with God. And God grieved. He searched desperately for His loved ones in the garden. He asked plaintively what they had done. And then, with His new creation crashing down around Him, God responded with self-sacrificial love. His plan was to sacrifice His Son to save and restore His precious people. God's love prevailed, for God is love.

This is why you invest yourself in people. This is why you pour yourself into life. You love because God first loved you. You take the risk because God risked it all for you. You share in God's suffering because it is the pathway to life that matters and means something. It is the pathway to revealing God's kindness, grace, righteousness, and eternal restoration. Trusting in God's eternal plan, you walk in His footsteps, knowing very well that you might lose your whole world here and now.

A SWORD AND A SEED

Jesus' mother was well acquainted with this grief. After her miraculous baby was born, Mary went with Joseph to the temple to have Him circumcised. Waiting there was Simeon, a godly man who was told by the Holy Spirit that he wouldn't die before he saw the Messiah. When the baby Jesus arrived, Simeon burst into song about the promised Savior. The waiting was over. But then Simeon said to Mary, "Behold, this child is appointed for the fall and rising of many in Israel, and for a sign that is opposed (and a sword will pierce through your own soul also)" (Luke 2:34–35).

Those are haunting words, but Simeon was right. Mary poured her love and care into the Son of God. For thirty years, she doted on Him, raised Him, taught Him, nurtured Him, saw Him become a strong young man, marveled at His knowledge and goodness, and then had to let Him go. She felt the sting of separation as the work of Jesus' heavenly Father took priority over His earthly family. Then Mary watched as Jesus was rejected, criticized, persecuted, tortured, and crucified. She was present when, on the cross, her bleeding, dying, and gasping Son said good-bye and asked the apostle John to care for her. The sword of loss pierced her soul. The sting of heartbreak wounded her spirit.

But God reveals that the risk of love is worth the cost because His love will change the worst losses into the greatest gains. Jesus rose from death. The sword that pierced Mary's soul became the key that opened the door for the salvation of the world.

You need to know that Jesus takes into His hands the losses that break your heart. The love you planted for years may very well grow to bear more fruit than you will ever realize. That's the goal, isn't it? Isn't the point of your love and passion the same as it was for Jesus? We're not here to revel in an earthly kingdom; we're here to lead people to the heavenly kingdom. Love leads the way there—God's love for you and His love through you. Any loss you suffer here is temporary. Yes, it hurts. The pain and heartbreak are beyond description. But life is always around the corner when your faith is centered in Jesus Christ, your Savior.

Consider Jesus' mother. After losing her son to an unjust crucifixion, we don't find Mary isolating herself in bitterness. She wasn't lost and alone. There was no sadness that swallowed her up or grief that crushed her completely. No, we find Mary, the mother of Jesus, in Acts 1, together with the disciples in Jerusalem, lifting up hopeful prayers. She was with her family and fellow believers, rejoicing in God's plan, awaiting the promised Holy Spirit, and preparing to become a strong witness of Jesus' resurrection to the world.

The risk is worth it. Pour your heart out, and be bold in showing God's love. Have no regrets as you face your grief. By God's grace, your investment will bear fruit that no loss can overcome.

Words for Healing

Devotion Guide for Chapter Fifty

READ Psalm 66

REFLECT

Psalm 66 tells of the journey of God's people—their love, their loss, and their blessing. How do verses 1–12 remind you of God's faithfulness through the ups and downs of your journey?

Verses 13–19 describe the worship and praise of someone looking back on life. As you look back at the love you invested, what benefit and blessing do you see?

As you see in verse 20, even as you experience sadness and loss, God is not rejecting you. In what ways has God encouraged you with His love and shown you His presence as you grieve?

PRAY a prayer of thanksgiving for the new life you see in the midst of sadness. Ask God to use the love and time you invested to bless and bear fruit. Ask for strength as you face a new and challenging season of life.

Love

WHEN THE SUN RISES AGAIN

The sunrise shall visit us from on high to give light to
those who sit in darkness and in the shadow of death, to
guide our feet into the way of peace. (Luke 1:78–79)

DAWN

You may have heard the saying "It's always darkest before the
dawn." No one is certain where that phrase originated, but its truth
seems to prove itself over and over again. A few years ago, I was driv-
ing through the night on my way to a wedding. The wee hours of the
morning ticked by slowly. The darkness made me weary and sleepy.
I knew that if I could make it until sunrise, I would be okay. After
fighting to stay awake and focused, the bright dawn on the horizon
brought new energy for the remainder of the journey. But those dark
hours were difficult. There were times I wondered if dawn would ever
come.

When heartbreak hits, dawn seems like an impossibility. Loss
can lay you so low, you may believe that you'll never again awaken
to see the light of day. Grief is so painful and may convince you that
darkness will never be dispelled.

But when you experience grief, you don't necessarily want it to
disappear. You don't want to forget your feelings. You don't want to
brush off the important loss in your life that led to your sadness. You
need to be in darkness for a while. You need to process and learn
and reflect and mourn. The pain of darkness is essential to the joy of
sunrise. But it sure would help to know when the dawn was coming.
That's the difficulty. When loss lingers, you wonder if you'll ever get
to the corner that has some joy waiting around the other side. You
begin to think that darkness is a permanent condition.

THE SUNRISE FROM HEAVEN

But each new day is a parable of what you are waiting for and
counting on as you travel through pain. Even after stretches of cloudy

and dreary weather, the sun will appear, piercing the darkness and spreading out warmly over the shadowy, cold world. Dawn comes again. It happens without your planning or efforts. The beauty may surprise you. It may stop you in your tracks so you can savor a look. Its bright reach may trigger a sense of peace and reset your hurried and worried defaults, showing you that simple beauty and brightness burst over the earth by the grace of God every day. After all, "The heavens declare the glory of God, and the sky above proclaims His handiwork. Day to day pours out speech, and night to night reveals knowledge. . . . Their voice goes out through all the earth, and their words to the end of the world. In them He has set a tent for the sun" (Psalm 19:1–2, 4).

Each sunrise is a promise from God that the sun will rise in your life again. And packed into that promise is the presence of Jesus, the Savior who defeated death, sadness, and gloom. Your darkness will not last forever. As you walk in faith, you have the certainty that an eternal sunrise is just over the horizon. Even now, its bright beams reach you with hope and strength through the gifts of God's Word and Sacraments.

When John the Baptist's father, Zechariah, sang a song of celebration about the birth of his son, he included a reference to Jesus. Zechariah sang, "And you, child, will be called the prophet of the Most High; for you will go before the Lord to prepare His ways, to give knowledge of salvation to His people in the forgiveness of their sins, because of the tender mercy of our God, whereby the sunrise shall visit us from on high to give light to those who sit in darkness and in the shadow of death, to guide our feet into the way of peace" (Luke 1:76–79).

Jesus was called "the sunrise." He would come to break all heartbreak once and for all. That's what Jesus has done for you. His resurrection has changed your grief. Jesus' defeat of death has an impact on your life—especially as you suffer loss. When Jesus rose from the dead, the bonds of death were broken. The power of death lost its permanence. Death is now just a passing evening before a bright eternal dawn. Your heartbreak and sadness are temporary. Yes, they hurt. True, they bring pain beyond any pain you've ever experienced. But your heartbreak and sadness suffer from the terminal illness of Jesus' resurrection. Their days are numbered. This is your hope. This is your strength as you travel through darkness. The dawn is coming.

THE KEYS

As you struggle to hold on, to stay focused, and to maintain hope on your drive through the darkness of loss, Jesus gives you the assurance that you are not at a standstill. You're heading toward the dawn, and your car will not die. In fact, Jesus gives you the certainty that He has the keys. In Revelation 1, the risen Christ appeared to the apostle John. Revealed in His glory and splendor, the Savior spoke of strength and comfort. Jesus said, "Fear not, I am the first and the last, and the living one. I died, and behold I am alive forevermore, and I have the keys of Death and Hades" (vv. 17–18).

Jesus has the keys. Your grief and pain are under His authority. In His resurrection from the dead, Jesus has taken the wheel and is in control of the vehicle. Grief is difficult and loss is disheartening, but by the grace of God through the compassionate sacrifice of His Son, you're bound for an eternal destination of hope and life. There will come a day when sadness will be a thing of the past, when grief will be no more, and when every broken heart will be fully healed. Even now, little seasons of relief come your way. Even now, God speaks strength into your life and blesses you with joy through His Word. And one day, the great day will come. The darkness will be pushed back, and eternal brightness will dawn in your heart. The apostle Paul said it this way: "When the perishable puts on the imperishable, and the mortal puts on immortality, then shall come to pass the saying that is written: 'Death is swallowed up in victory' " (1 Corinthians 15:54).

Yes, look for it. Look for the sunrise, and see the lasting hope of restoration through your risen Savior.

WORDS FOR HEALING
Devotion Guide for Chapter Fifty-One

READ Psalm 19:1–8

REFLECT

Verses 1–6 laud the majesty of God's creation and the tenacity of the rising sun. How does the certainty of the sunrise give you hope for your future?

What do verses 7–8 tell you about the effect of God's Word on your broken heart?

How does God revive your soul on a regular basis, and how does His promise of eternal restoration cause your heart to rejoice?

PRAY for God's help and hope as you navigate the darkness of grief. Ask Him to show you bright beams of dawn as you struggle with loss. Thank Him for His promises, and let Him know how you need to be sustained right now.

Hope for a New Season
WHEN YOUR GRIEF COMPANION
BEGINS TO TAKE A BACK SEAT

But Joseph said to [his brothers], "Do not fear, for am I
in the place of God? As for you, you meant evil against
me, but God meant it for good. . . . So do not fear; I will
provide for you and your little ones." (Genesis 50:19–21)

THE BEGINNING

Be sure you don't read this chapter too soon. If you're going to
read it, you need to wait until you've experienced a day—or even a
few moments—when you forgot your sadness. Yes, you need to read
this chapter when you are looking back at your grief more than when
you are staring it in the face.

It will take a while to get to this point. Your heartbreak won't get
into the back seat of your life willingly or eagerly. It will only end up
there when it is crowded out of the front seat by time, God's grace,
prayer, Jesus' hope and presence, love from people in your life, little
miracles of God (and sometimes big ones), a few quarts of tears, a
whole load of meaningful Bible verses, some sleepless nights, some
long conversations, and even a few rants.

One day, you'll not only feel normal again, but you'll be excited
about something. You'll be able to look back at your grief without
crying—at least once in a while. You may even see a glimpse of God's
purpose in your pain.

When that happens, you'll know that your grief companion is
being tired out and worn down by God's tenacious help and healing.
You'll realize that God has been chasing after you, pursuing you with
determination and unrelenting love. Heartbreak will always be hanging around somewhere, but instead of being overcome with anguish,
you'll be filled with wisdom and compassion. You will possess a new
spirit of empathy and will approach people with patient understanding. Your heart will no longer be torn by grief but seasoned by it. You
will sense a new beginning.

NEW LIFE

Joseph experienced that unexpected miracle as the years unfolded and as God showed His faithfulness. Life was never completely the same after his suffering and loss. Joseph never did get to go back home. He stayed in Egypt and lived a life he never anticipated. But God blessed Him and took care of Him. God gave Him purpose and walked with him.

That's what God does when life is disrupted by heartbreak. When grief barges in and changes everything for the worse, God gets involved and turns brokenness into blessing.

Joseph's brothers thought that once their father died, Joseph would pay them back for their evil. They came to Joseph and begged for leniency, telling him they would be his slaves. But Joseph spoke to them kindly and said, "Do not fear, for am I in the place of God? As for you, you meant evil against me, but God meant it for good." Many lives were saved because of Joseph's presence in Egypt. Helping the world through a famine wasn't the task to which Joseph aspired, but after decades of struggling and sadness, Joseph embraced God's leadership for his life.

I don't believe you would have chosen to experience your grief. The heartbreak you've endured would never show up on any wish list for your life. But if you can spot some blessing that has been born because of it, if you can see one life that benefited because of your struggle, you can say with Joseph, "I thought my sadness was pure evil, but God meant it for good."

GRIEF'S WEAKNESS, GOD'S STRENGTH

Grief is always a wild ride. It lasts much too long and hurts far too severely. It is unpredictable in its effects and surprising in its depths. It defies patterns and has no regard for time. It will outlast the reading of this book, but it cannot outlast the reach of your Savior.

Because Jesus died and rose again to forgive sins, to defeat death, to bring you hope and restoration, and to bless you with eternal life, grief gets tired. It gets old and run down. Because of God's kindness, time is grace. Grief cannot stand the test of time when God is operating the clock. Grief seems so strong when it roars with punishing gusto on the day it comes into being. Loss looms so large when it grabs hold of you in its heyday. But let some time pass. When treated regularly with the steadfast love of God in Jesus Christ, grief is ready for the rest home. Perhaps that's why it tries so hard at the beginning; it knows its days are numbered. There are times when grief cannot even get out of diapers before the Shepherd of our souls puts it out to pasture. That's why you never need to look into the eyes of grief with terror. You can always stare down grief with great hope.

More than that, God commandeers grief and uses it as an instrument of His grace. That's startlingly audacious, isn't it? I was watching a television show that told the story of a grief-stricken family. As they gathered somberly around the dinner table one evening, the father reflected on their loss and realized, like Joseph, that God was using it painfully for their good. He quoted a favorite line from Aeschylus (ancient Greek dramatist) to his family: "Even in our sleep, pain which cannot forget falls drop by drop upon the heart until, in our own despair, against our will, comes wisdom through the awful grace of God." With bold and daring abandon, God plunges into heartbreak and bursts forth with its wild and thrashing tail in His hand to work abiding and holy transformation in your life.

You may be ready to hear that. You may not. You may be able to see a glimpse of God's gifts in your grief. Or your heartbreak may be too tender. But please know this: as you navigate your season of loss, your loving God will give you the gift of His enduring and eternal hope. That hope is not a personal character trait you possess. It is a person. Your hope is Jesus. He is strength and life no loss can overcome. He is with you. Jesus will always be your hope when your heart breaks.

WORDS FOR HEALING
Devotion Guide for Chapter Fifty-Two

READ Isaiah 61:1–3

REFLECT

Jesus quoted these words and applied them to Himself in Luke 4:16–21. How have you seen this work of Jesus in your life?

What good news have you been blessed with and encouraged by during your reading of this book?

How has your journey of grief equipped you to help others?

PRAY that God would bring you His Good News every day, that He would bind up your broken heart, that He would free you from the pain of grief, and that He would comfort you as you mourn. Thank God for sending Jesus to bring the beauty of His grace to life even in the midst of hurt and sadness.

SCRIPTURE INDEX